Field o' My Dreams

Gene Stratton-Porter in 1924.
Courtesy of the Indiana State Library.

Field o' My Dreams
The Poetry of Gene Stratton-Porter

Compiled and Edited by
Mary DeJong Obuchowski

THE KENT STATE
UNIVERSITY PRESS
Kent, Ohio

© 2007 by the Kent State University Press, Kent, Ohio 44242
ALL RIGHTS RESERVED
Library of Congress Catalog Card Number 2006037405

ISBN: 978-0-87338-902-0

Manufactured in the United States of America

11 10 09 08 07   5 4 3 2 1

Library of Congress Cataloging-in-Publication Data

Stratton-Porter, Gene, 1863–1924.
Field o' my dreams : the poetry of Gene Stratton-Porter / compiled and
edited by Mary DeJong Obuchowski.
    p. cm.
Includes bibliographical references (p.   ).
    ISBN 978-0-87338-902-0 (alk. paper) ∞
    I. Obuchowski, Mary DeJong, 1940– II. Title. III. Title: Field of my
    dreams.
PS3531.O7345F48 2007
811'.52—dc22   2006037405

British Library Cataloging-in-Publication data are available.

To Pete, without whom this would not have been possible.

Contents

Acknowledgments

Many people and organizations have contributed time, thought, and expertise to the process of developing this book. I wish to express my gratitude to many, including my parents, Madge and Russell DeJong, whose gifts and encouragement helped to begin my study of Gene Stratton-Porter; Central Michigan University for two sabbatical leaves and a Faculty Research and Creative Endeavors grant; the knowledgeable and invaluable David G. MacLean for getting the project started, and for extensive editing of early versions and advising; the Society for the Study of Midwestern Literature, particularly David D. and Patricia Anderson, Marilyn Atlas, and Philip A. Greasley; Central Michigan's Clarke Historical Collection and Interlibrary Loan, now Document Access, for repeated and extensive help; John and James Meehan, Gene Stratton-Porter's grandsons, for allowing access and permission to publish the manuscripts, and to Monica Berg, her great-granddaughter, for continuing and enlarging their help; Deborah Dahlke for sharing the manuscripts; Anastasia Clothier Hathaway for generous conversations about her great-aunt; Bertrand Richards and Sydney Landon Plum, for generosity with their research and ideas; the staff at the Indiana State Memorials at Geneva and Rome City; John Krug; the Indiana State Library; the Indiana State Historical Society; Indiana University Lilly Library; the Geneva Public Library; Carnegie Library in Wabash; the Fort Wayne Public Library; Ronald R. Primeau for setting me in the right direction; Joanna Hildebrand Craig; and especially my husband, who read every version and made this book much better than it would otherwise have been; and my sons Tim and John for their patience and support. If, with all of this assistance, there are errors of fact, omission, or transcription, the responsibility lies with me.

Introduction

Readers of Gene Stratton-Porter know her best as an immensely popular novelist of the first quarter of the twentieth century, whose *Freckles* (1904), *A Girl of the Limberlost* (1909), and other novels continue to be reprinted for enthusiastic readers.[1] Recently more attention has been given to the facts that she also pioneered as a nature photographer as well as a writer and an activist, that she became an influential magazine columnist, that she produced films based on her novels, and that she built houses—besides being a wife and mother. In addition to those aspects of her life, she was a poet whose verse, until now, has all but slipped into obscurity. A few poems appeared in magazines. She used others as captions in a lyrical work of nonfiction, *Music of the Wild* (1910). Poems make up about one-third of one of her books for children, *Morning Face* (1916). Two were published as beautifully bound and illustrated books in limited editions: *The Fire Bird* in 1922 and *Jesus of the Emerald* in 1923. And the long narrative "Euphorbia" was serialized in *Good Housekeeping*, also in 1923. It has recently become clear that Porter apparently intended to present a collection of her poems to her public, but that act was precluded by her untimely death in 1924.

In theme and style, Porter's fiction and nonfiction are consistent throughout her career. Her appreciation of nature, her awe at its creator, her desire to infuse readers with her enthusiasm for it, her concern for others, especially women and children, and her drive to reform: all of these inform her prose. They dominate her poetry as well, but in terms of form and innovation, the poetry matures as the woman does.

Gene Stratton-Porter was born Geneva Grace Stratton August 17, 1863, on a farm in LaGro Township, Wabash County, Indiana, to a father who was a Methodist preacher in addition to being a farmer, and to a mother who excelled at growing flowers.[2] The last of twelve children, she seems to have benefited from a freedom not allowed her older siblings, for she spent as much time as possible outdoors, taking special pleasure in observing domestic plants and animals and wildlife, especially birds. She learned to approach them quietly so that she could learn their nesting and feeding habits, and even rescued injured ones, inducing her mother to call her "a little bird woman."[3] She became particularly attuned to the seasons and to the geography of the place, elements which pervade both her prose and poetry.

Geneva hated school and resisted formal education, both at the country school where she began, and in the city of Wabash, where her family lived beginning in 1874.[4] She writes,

> I was placed in the public schools of the nearest county seat, and an effort [was] made to instill Latin, Greek, and calculus. In the whole of my school life I never had one teacher who made the slightest effort to discover what I cared for personally, what I had been born to do, or who made any attempt to help me in any direction I evinced an inclination to develop. I was to be pushed into the groove in which all other pupils ran. When I could not be forced, it was because I was of poor mentality or had a bad disposition.[5]

Still, she read the books in their house and began writing poetry in her childhood, perhaps impelled by her father's recitation of Bible passages from memory and by dramatic readings from prose and poetry.[6] For the entertainment of her family, she wrote and acted out poems before she even began school; her daughter, Jeannette Porter Meehan, describes a few such performances in her biography of Porter.[7] Meehan also reports on an incident in which her mother was assigned a paper on "Mathematical Law," but what she turned in was a recounting of the story in Xavier Boniface Saintine's *Picciola*. She read it aloud to a surprised but mesmerized audience of pupils and teachers.[8] This event reflects both her love of reading and writing and her rebellion against restrictions and authority, particularly in school.

Writing compelled her from her earliest memories; in an autobiographical article, she notes,

> I cannot remember the time when I was not tugging at my mother's apron, begging her to "set down" things which I thought were stories and poems. I was literally pushed and driven, so that I found

an outlet by slipping away alone, to recite these efforts from im-provised platforms on the fences, trees, and in the barn loft, or by delivering impromptu orations on almost every feature of our ev-eryday life. In this, I found unspeakable delight.[9]

She adds, "When I was supposed to be laboring over Greek and geo-metry, I wrote a book of poetry, two books of fiction, and many stories, all of which I destroyed later, and now fervently wish that I had not."[10] In an undated letter to the poet and translator Dr. Charles Wharton Stork, per-haps in response to a letter on her 1922 poem, "Euphorbia," she expands on that regret, remembering,

> When I sacrificed my first three efforts at poetry, I was the victim of some extremely ill-advised advice from a person upon whose judg-ment I had the misfortune to rely utterly. . . . Yet as the years rolled along, and I had some small success with writing other things, the poetry virus still worked in me often, and I never missed an oppor-tunity of purchasing a book and studying deeply the laws of poetry, the efforts of the poets of different nations.

She further asserts, "I shall never forget the dumbfounded feeling that took possession of my heart and brain when in reply to my direct question to you as to whether I could write poetry, you made me reply, 'My dear lady, you have never written anything else!'"[11]

During her school yeasrs, Geneva's name changed to Geneve, and by the time of her marriage, she had shortened it to Gene.[12] She never fin-ished high school, although she took music and painting lessons, and at-tended chautauquas at Sylvan Lake, near Rome City, Indiana. At one of these events, a pharmacist named Charles Dorwin Porter noticed her and, using his acquaintance with some of her relatives, began to corre-spond with her in 1884. He visited her in Wabash the next year, and three months later they became engaged.

They married in April 1886, living first in Decatur, between his drug-stores in Fort Wayne and Geneva, Indiana, and then, in 1888, in Geneva. By that time they had a baby, Jeannette. During her early years in Ge-neva, Gene joined a literary organization for women. For one of its meet-ings, she reviewed Walt Whitman's *Leaves of Grass,* praising its spiritual values, appreciation of nature, and "the pulse of his rhythm and song."[13] His rhythmic cadences echo in her later poetry.

At about the same time, she began writing about birds, and for illustrations took up photography. The nearby Limberlost Swamp and Wabash River provided her with abundant subjects; the patience she learned as a child helped her in the long waits with the glass plates and exposures required for turn-of-the-century cameras. She also learned more about the nature and habits of wildlife, particularly of birds. She must have been an extraordinary sight, dressed in "a knee-length khaki skirt with high leather hiking boots, a blouse or sweater of either brown or green, which blended with the outdoor colours, and a hat to match. She carried a revolver for protection."[14] Later photographs show her in trousers. By 1900 this field-work had provided material for her first publications, articles in *Recreation* magazine, many of them for a column called "Camera Notes." She quickly branched out, finding more venues for her wildlife articles as well as her short stories. Her first book, *The Song of the Cardinal* (1903), combines nature study with fiction. Discovery of a black vulture in the Limberlost provided her with numerous photographs, several articles, and a portion of the plot of *Freckles*, one of her most successful novels. She followed *Freckles* with several more books of both fiction and nonfiction, and her articles continued to appear in a variety of magazines. Her work from this period leaves a visual and verbal record of her childhood perceptions of the Midwestern farm and wilderness landscapes, with their plants and animals. The values with which she grew up—hard work, upright behavior, regard for the needs of others, spiritual belief, and independence of thought and action—come through in the fiction and the nature books. The added dimension of concern for the fate of the forests, swamps, and meadows and the flora and fauna that inhabited them made her an early activist in the conservation movement.

As her husband Charles prospered, going into banking while an oil boom enriched the area, Porter designed a new house in Geneva for the family and called it Limberlost Cabin. An impressive, roomy structure of Wisconsin cedar logs, it has become an Indiana state memorial site. However, the lumbering interests that provided a setting for *Freckles* were already deforesting the Limberlost. The best trees went to furniture factories in Grand Rapids, Michigan, and the rest for lumber; then the oil interests moved in. Finally, the swamp was drained for farmland.

Though it was a source of her husband's wealth, drilling for oil ruined the Limberlost and thus a major source of nature and photography for Gene Stratton-Porter. Therefore, with earnings from her books, she built a second house on Sylvan Lake, near Rome City, Indiana. She called her new home both Limberlost North and Wildflower Woods, the latter because she made the grounds into a kind of nature preserve by transplanting as many native plants as she could there. It, too, was later named a state memorial site. By 1920 she had moved to Los Angeles, in part for reasons of health, in part to supervise the filming of some of her novels, and in part because of hardships imposed by World War I in finding employees and coal. She formed and ran her own film company, built more houses in the Los Angeles area, and began writing monthly columns for *McCall's*. Concurrently, she was providing a series of articles for *Good Housekeeping* and completing and publishing four additional novels and three long poems. At the time of her sudden death in an automobile accident on December 6, 1924, there were more manuscripts ready to go. Two books, *The Keeper of the Bees* (1925) and *Tales You Won't Believe* (1925), the poem "Whitmore's Bull" (1926), and dozens of articles were scheduled to appear. Later, her daughter found a manuscript of one more novel, *The Magic Garden* (1927), and put together a book of essays culled from her magazine articles, *Let Us Highly Resolve* (1927).

For the first decade of her writing career, Porter published mainly prose: novels, nature books lavishly illustrated with her photographs, short fiction, and magazine articles. She branched out into poetry and later film. In total, she wrote twelve novels, six works of nonfiction, two long poems as books, two volumes for children, and scores of articles, stories, and poems for magazines. Her film company issued seven of her novels as movies. Still, because so much of her writing consisted of prose, many readers assume that prose was her preferred medium. It appears, however, that even in her fiction, poetry was always in her mind. She maintained:

I like to strive for smooth, musical, effective results. I like paragraphs that swing through a story with a rhythmic sweep. I have juggled with sentences for days, and taken them to bed with me at night, in an effort to combine music with truth and realism. All this work was not without its reward, for half of the criticisms of my first book called it a "prose poem."[5]

As far as can be discovered, Porter's first published poetry appeared in 1910. A prose book on the landscapes surrounding her home, *Music of the Wild*, included brief poems as captions to the multitude of photographs that illustrated it. Some of those poems are attributed to well-known poets, but the rest, which are not attributed, resemble Porter's other poems in their language, versification, and content.

"A Limberlost Invitation" was Porter's first poem to appear under her own name. It welcomes readers to the area celebrated in a book compiled by George Ade, *An Invitation to You and Your Folks from Jim and Some More of the Home Folks*, published in 1916 for the Indiana State Historical Commission by Bobbs-Merrill.

For *Morning Face* (1916), Porter put together a collection of photographs, stories, and poems for children in honor of her first granddaughter. At that time, however, she denied that she wrote poetry; indeed, her "Publisher's Note" baldly states, "Mrs. Porter makes no slightest claim to being a poet, or that many of the subjects of this book are poetical. It merely represents her methods of entertaining and teaching natural history to the babies of her own family."[16] The lessons and humor in *Morning Face* go a long way toward fulfilling these goals.

In 1919 Porter placed "Peter's Flowers" in *The Red Cross Magazine,* and "Symbols" and "Blue-eyed Mary" in *Good Housekeeping* in 1921. *The Fire Bird* and *Jesus of the Emerald* were issued in 1922 and 1923, respectively, and "Euphorbia" started serially in *Good Housekeeping* also in 1923. Two more poems appeared in magazines after that, "Field o' My Dreams" in *Outdoor America* in 1924 and "Whitmore's Bull" posthumously in *McCall's* in 1926. The rest of her poems, to her family's knowledge, remained among her daughter's papers until they were opened to an outsider, Deborah Dahlke-Scott, some years after Jeannette's death in 1971.

During her lifetime, Porter experienced immense change and progress, both in her immediate environment and in the greater world around her. She was born during the Civil War, in which her antislavery family seems to have escaped direct involvement. Her parents may have offered shelter to runaway slaves.[17] She wrote favorably of childhood experiences with the Native American Potawotamies, Miamis, and Meshingmesas in rural Indiana.[18] Many years later, in California, her acquaintance with photographer Edward Curtis and his dramatic portraits revived those memories and inspired her to write *The Fire Bird,* which celebrates Native American ways of life while condemning its protagonist to a fate commensurate with her jealous acts.[19]

Agricultural and industrial development was transforming Indiana in the same way as it was the rest of the country. The railroad increased trade and provided greater markets for agriculture and industry. As an adult,

Porter observed and recorded the changes to the Limberlost which drove her to a less spoiled area in the northern part of the state. Later she visited Hopewell Farm, her childhood home, and found the creeks and streams gone, the land altered almost beyond recognition. Despite her knowledge of the changing world, by and large her writing reflects relative isolation from pervasive national and world events, with a few exceptions.

World War I touched Porter profoundly. In a long letter to friends in Scotland, she writes,

> The war has been a terror from the beginning, and now that it is taking our nearest and dearest, it comes home with a new meaning. . . . When I read that a battle is raging at Toul, and think of my sister's son Donald, in aviation there, to all I felt before is now added the deadly chill of apprehension that no one can know, until their own *flesh and blood are in it* [Porter's italics].[20]

Porter, her family, and her employees did some war work, mainly knitting. Some of her male workers were enlisted at that time, and she suffered from a shortage of help.[21] However, for all of her emotional involvement, she published relatively little about the war. "Peter's Flowers," a 1919 poem, mourns the death of a young American buried in Flanders Field. It may be compared to Canadian John McCrae's immensely popular "In Flanders Fields" (1915), which also speaks on behalf of those who died in battle. The great difference between her poem and those by writers who were actually present is that McCrae, Wilfrid Owen, Siegfried Sassoon, and the other soldier poets record and express the tragedy and ironies of the war in tones that reflect the strain on their bodies and minds, the internal and external conflicts, and the brutality of war. Porter's narrator describes the same fields that McCrae's does, but grieves with a gentle sorrow that recalls the beauty of the flowers and of the boy who died, without the anger, desperation, and horror of the poets who had been in battle. There is no actual evidence that Porter had read her contemporaries' war poetry, though she may very well have done so, particularly "In Flanders Fields." Porter's only novel to deal with World War I, *The Keeper of the Bees* (1925), does so indirectly by telling the story of how a wounded soldier finds healing through nature. Thus, the events of the war seem relatively distant in the context of her work. Nevertheless, a war-related consequence of her books, particularly her novels, turns up in her correspondence: she received quantities of appreciative letters from both men and women, including military personnel who ranged "from admirals on the North Sea watch, down through Majors, captains, and lieutenants to the men in the trenches and on battleships . . . all bearing the message that my books have helped them to meet life with braver front, to be cleaner, kinder men, to find a new joy they never before have known in the outdoors."[22]

In her prose, she comments on shifts in physical and social attitudes closer to home. Her poetry reflects these changes in more subtle ways: with nostalgia for the birds, meadows, and woods of her childhood; and with concern for the impingement of modernism on human morals, values, physical health, and spiritual well-being. In those ways, she looks back toward some of the American Romantics, who, with Emerson, tended to elevate the role and beauty of landscape. Sharing the practical and realistic treatment of the details of nature with Thoreau, she idealizes him in fiction in the person of David Langston, the Harvester. She was aware of the literary realism of her day, but her works cannot profitably be compared with those of such authors as Sherwood Anderson or Carl Sandburg. Indeed, in the case of her first successful novel, *Freckles*, she said that although she had intended "another book of woodlore, straight nature stuff through which [she] ran a slight romance as a sugar coating," in order "to entice the housebound afield," she had also intended a realistic conclusion, saying, "I named it 'The Falling Feather,' and it ended where the tree fell and crushed 'Freckles.'"[23] Her publishers, however, refused the book unless it had the positive resolution characteristic of the then current popular mode.[24] *Freckles* had tremendous sales, and she never plotted a tragic ending to a novel again. In rewarding the virtues of her protagonists, she reveals her affinity with the American Victorians in their didacticism and morality. When criticized for sentimentality, she justified her plots by saying, "It is true that I write almost altogether of the *best* I know of human nature and deliberately leave the worst to those who enjoy reproducing it."[25] Although their emphasis on nature continues to engage readers, to some extent the love stories, idealism, and conventional endings were all part of the formula for her overwhelming popularity during her lifetime, and both qualities—the descriptions of the outdoors and the formulaic matters—continue to draw an audience in the twenty-first century.

On the other hand, in her late columns in *McCall's*, which appeared from 1922 through 1927, she takes up such social issues as family relationships, education, politics, various aspects of morality, providing information about sex to children, comfortable clothing for women, and censorship of films.

In her late novel, *The White Flag* (1923), in which events focus on some of the darker aspects of small-town life, and in the poems *The Fire Bird* and "Euphorbia," she takes on themes of jealousy, murder, alcoholism, spousal abuse, and the hardships imposed by the early years of the Dust Bowl, linking herself in those cases more closely to the Realists. In the late quartet of poems, the cycle of the seasons beginning with "Desire" (representing spring), followed by "Fulfillment" and "Apprehension," and ending with "Abandonment," Porter takes the uncharacteristic step of expressing frankly the sexual attraction between males and females on one level, while also following the stages of life from before conception to death. With the exception of these darker works, she maintains the standard positive outcomes for the main characters.

This optimistic stance corresponds with her spiritual outlook. Though reared in a Methodist household, which required regular churchgoing, daily prayer, and language free of profanity, she did not attend church as an adult. In fact, she announces, "If possible, I would advocate holding services out-of-doors in summer, giving as my reason that God so manifests Himself in the trees, flowers, and grass, that to be among His creations puts one in a devotional frame of mind, gives better air to breathe, and puts worship on a natural basis, as it was in the beginning, when Christ taught the people beside the sea and in the open."[26] She did, however, maintain clean language, and her writing is full of grateful invocations of a spiritual presence.

In her 1909 nature book, *Birds of the Bible*, she approaches her topic from the perspective of a historian and a nature lover as well as of a person with strong religious belief, noting that worship occurs in cultures throughout the world.[27] In most of her books and articles on birds, moths, and other flora and fauna, she often refers to God, expressing thanksgiving and wonder that such things of beauty have been created.[28] Clearly, nature aroused an awareness of what in *Music of the Wild* she variously calls "God," "the Creator," "the Almighty," and "the Infinite." In the same book she quotes William Cullen Bryant more than once, and shares his spiritual affinity for nature, comparing the forest "with a place of worship," describing the woods as full of altars and the sound of wind in the trees as organ music.[29] Several of the protagonists in her novels—notably those most deeply affected by nature, including David Langston in *The Harvester*, Freckles, and Jamie MacFarlane in *The Keeper of the Bees* (1925)—engage in spontaneous prayer and praise. Porter, herself, also invokes Biblical teachings in the *McCall's* articles which by and large discuss how human beings treat each other.[30] In the poetry, references to the spiritual abound. Porter expresses thanksgiving and worship in many of the nature poems. For example, "Symbols" suggests both a sacred source of flowers, butterflies, and birds and their capacity for inspiring religious thoughts. "Field o' My Dreams" calls spring beauty "God's promise," and also warns that anyone who wantonly rips out wildflowers "Sins a sin that knows no pardon, against the God of all things growing!" In a more philosophical vein, the previously unpublished "The Wine of Life Pitcher" represents a discussion between "Life" and a "Master Potter" on the proportions of joy and sorrow measured out to each human being; and "Heart of the World" suggests that the extremes of personality and emotion appear in people throughout the world.

The long narrative poems offer more eclectic religious positions. Yiada, the narrator of *The Fire Bird*, angers the "Great Spirit" by making three attempts, the final one successful, to kill her rival, Coüy-oüy. In recompense, the Great Spirit subjects each of Yiada's three children to the kinds of death she planned for Coüy-oüy. In *Jesus of the Emerald*, Porter makes her most explicit, and at the same time most ecumenical, religious statement of her career. Her long "Afterword" explains not only the legend of the emerald on which Jesus's face is supposed to be carved, but reflects the extensive research she put into documenting the existence of the emerald she describes. In fact, reports of such an engraved stone were in circulation during the time between the publication of *Birds of the Bible* and *Jesus of the Emerald*.[31] Drawing together her religious and scientific theories, she iterates her belief in the universality of spiritual faiths and their many similarities across the world and in salvation. In "Euphorbia" she returns to more conventional, though emphatic, expressions of faith with a number of references to prayer.

Music of the Wild establishes Porter's familiarity with the world of poetry. Under the numerous photographs in the prose book, about half of the captions come from the poems of Anacreon, William Shakespeare, the Romantics, and Victorians such as George Gordon, Lord Byron, and Alfred, Lord Tennyson; and among American poets, she includes John Greenleaf Whittier, Henry Wadsworth Longfellow, and Ralph Waldo Emerson.

The paper that Porter wrote during the early years of her marriage, and her later poem on Walt Whitman, show how deeply she was touched by Whitman's life and attitudes toward nature. Even more, his long lines and rhythms echoing air and water movement clearly inspired Porter to find her own cadences that mimic wind, waves, birdsongs, and emotions, particularly in *The Fire Bird* and "Euphorbia." It is likely that Longfellow's "Hiawatha" also may have had some influence on *The Fire Bird* in her use of a Native American legend as a basis for its plot and in some of its rhythms and phrasing. Porter's repeated line, "Where the triumphant blue sea water" (25 and elsewhere), for example, echoes the opening of "Hiawatha." Her repetition and parallelism also call Longfellow's techniques to mind.

In keeping up with the culture of her time, Porter was outraged by some of its aspects such as jazz, "modern dancing," and E. E. Cummings's iconoclasm, railing against the liberties he took with capitalization, spacing, and meter.[32] There was much that she approved, however. She was familiar with at least some of the literary publications of the time, such as her friend Dr. Stork's quarterly *Contemporary Verse*. In a *McCall's* editorial, Porter conveys her awareness and enthusiasm for the innovative literature swirling around the United States and Europe during the early years of the twentieth century, encouraging her readers to read widely. She praises Vachel Lindsay's verse, particularly his poem "General Booth Enters into Heaven," asserting, "If I can enter Heaven for myself, just once, anywhere near as naturally as I have entered times unnumbered with General Booth, I shall be fortunate. Lindsay is a great help in the problem of daily living." In the same article, she also admires Mary Austin, exclaiming that *The American Rhythm* is "about the life we live in this great land of ours—the song of the axe stroke, the sweep of the scythe, the hum of life where it strikes in measured rhythms that I have heard all my life."[33]

Porter's principal biographer, her daughter Jeannette Meehan, quotes an undated letter to Harriet Monroe in which Porter states that she had enjoyed Monroe's poem "Supernal Dialogue" and that she was sending Monroe a copy of *Jesus of the Emerald*, but there is no record of a response.[34] Meehan also includes a 1915 letter from James Whitcomb Riley, whom Meehan refers to as "the beloved Riley."[35] This suggests that Porter enjoyed his poetry as much as her fellow Hoosiers did. His poems may have given her license to use the dialect that appears in her novels and poetry, notably the poems in *Morning Face*. Her work falls somewhere between the Romantics' elevation of nature and Riley's homespun warmth, with different ranges of subject and mode than the poetry of either.

By 1920 Porter had a volume of poetry ready for publication, including the verses published in magazines and several others. One wonders why the project never came to fruition. Perhaps, as some of her letters suggest, she lacked confidence in herself as a poet in 1920. She writes to Dr. Stork, "I have wasted a thousand things as fine as 'The Wine Pitcher' [see "The Wine of Life Pitcher" in this volume] in the past twenty years because I thought they were no good."[36] Her projected volume of verses might have solidified her reputation as a poet. Still, in an article in the *Los Angeles Times* in 1922 on *The Fire Bird,* she is quoted as saying, "For years . . . I have wanted to write poetry. But my publishers always assured me that poetry would never pay. I stood it as long as I could, and then I 'bust loose.'"[37] Whether reticence, the pressure of her other work, the attitude of her publishers, or for some other reason, why Porter never finished that final volume of poems may never be known. Nevertheless, she did "bust loose" with two more long poems that made highly public appearances in the next year. The 1923 publication of *Jesus of the Emerald* and "Euphorbia" should have solidified her reputation as a poet, but along with her other poetry and nonfiction, they remain largely forgotten.

Thematically, the poems form a fundamental part of Gene Stratton-Porter's total writing. The consistency of their content shows that they are part of a unified body of work among themselves and with her fiction and nonfiction.

Appreciation of nature underlies the plots in Porter's fiction. Her nonfiction books and nature articles also embody reverence for ancient forests and delight in the beauty of flowers, birds, and moths. Similarly, her work expresses gratitude for the food, medicine, and emotional and spiritual benefits that nature provides. For example, in *Jesus of the Emerald* an artisan considers a number of gems in deciding which one he will use for a carving of Christ's face. The description of each jewel contains a portion devoted to plants and animals; the fact that the inorganic gems bring to mind living things enhances them in the Master Craftsman's mind and inevitably associates them with Christ. There is a similar religious quality in the appreciation that David Langston in *The Harvester,* the friends in *At the Foot of the Rainbow,* and the narrator of "Whitmore's Bull" transmit, directly or indirectly, for spring. Flowers are central in "Peter's Flowers" and "Blue-eyed Mary" as well as many of the poems in *Music of the Wild* and *Morning Face.* Blooming plants also figure brilliantly in the novel *The Keeper of the Bees.* An article, "No Lazy Man Can Make a Garden," enumerates flowers that provide "mental and moral uplift."[38] "The Healing Influence of Gardens" explains the benefits for both adults and children of cultivating flowers.[39]

Moths, birds, trees, herbs, the ocean, cultivated plants, and bees affect the characters, as well as the plots and concepts, in both Porter's prose and the poetry. For example, the protagonists of the poem "Euphorbia" and the novel *Her Father's Daughter* focus important elements of their lives on the plants of the California mountains and coast, and some actions center around those plants. In the novel, Linda Strong makes a name (or rather, a pen name) for herself by writing and illustrating magazine articles about the edible flora of the region. Transplanting wildflowers affords Marge Travers of "Euphorbia" satisfaction that she is unable to achieve from her marriage to a brutal husband. Attitude toward flowering plants even becomes a test of character and a source of doom for Jacob Travers, who has tortured Marge by trampling and pulling up her cherished plants. One of these plants is the euphorbia, which is said to cure snakebites. When later intoxicated by the bootleg "white mule" and thinking a snake has bitten him, Jacob cannot find the medicinal plant to save himself and dies. Marge also uses plants for landscaping and for their potential healing qualities, as does David Langston in *The Harvester*. *The Keeper of the Bees* also makes a point about the California coast and its healthful attributes, most notably the fresh fruits and vegetables it produces, as well as its sunshine and salt water, which all help to heal Jamie MacFarlane's body. In that book, Jamie and his young friend called Little Scout (the characters who love plants and bees) prevail over the person who has no respect for them, an imposter who tries to inherit her estranged stepfather's property.

Those characters who abuse nature meet with unpleasant, sometimes fatal, consequences, in Porter's novels and poems. Jimmy Malone, in *At the Foot of the Rainbow*, neglects both his muskrat traps and his garden in favor of drinking in town; he dies from alcoholism, as does the unsavory Jacob Travers of "Euphorbia." In *The Fire Bird*, Yiada twists the purposes of nature in her attempts to kill her rival and endures parallel consequences.

Porter's empathy for the human inhabitants of her fictional world intertwines with her devotion to nature. Mahala Jackson in *The White Flag* and Coüy-oüy in *The Fire Bird* portray the appreciative, nurturing qualities so often apparent in her female protagonists. The main characters Kate Bates (*A Daughter of the Land*) and Marge Travers ("Euphorbia") stand up for their rights as women. Porter's monthly magazine articles, which appeared for six years in *McCall's*, also reflect many social concerns present in the poetry. She repeatedly advised respect between husbands and wives in those columns, and provided models of its necessity in *Michael O'Halloran, At the Foot of the Rainbow,* and *A Daughter of the Land,* among others.[40] Further, in *McCall's,* she urged such humane improvements as labor-saving devices in the kitchen, which were lacking in the houses of Peter and Nancy Harding in *Michael O'Halloran* and of the Traverses in "Euphorbia."[41] In the articles, she also rages against abuses, including the neglect of children.[42] Such damaging acts show up in the poetry and the fiction as well. Parents fail their children, born and unborn, in "Euphorbia," *A Girl of the Limberlost, A Daughter of the Land,* and *Michael O'Halloran.*

Porter also encouraged concern for one's neighbor, which is implied not only in *The Harvester,* when David Langston provides a gentle burial for his indigent mother-in-law, and in *Michael O'Halloran,* where the issue is care for a severely handicapped orphan, but also in the short poems "Heart of the World" and "The Wine of Life Pitcher." Further, one *McCall's* article is titled "Am I My Brother's Keeper?" She concurrently advocates worship of a creator, as expressed in "Symbols," "Our Lord's Candles," and *Jesus of the Emerald,* as well as by characters in *A Daughter of the Land, Keeper of the Bees,* and other novels.

As Porter's themes became richer, her poetic technique matured during her later years. She made it clear that she had studied prosody over a period of time and considered it carefully in her writing. Earlier criticism of her verses had stung her severely, causing her to discard those first efforts. To Dr. Stork she explains:

> I was told that writing poetry was primarily a gift from God; secondarily, the result of years of deep study, which I had not had, and had neither books nor opportunity at that time to attain. Such words as "hexameter" and "pentameter" were hurled at my unprotected head until in despair I gave up any idea of ever being able to write poetry. . . . And when the day and the hour came that some poetic conception took form in my brain to such an extent that it was of no use for anything else, I wrote it and hid it.[43]

Nevertheless, her confidence grew, and many years afterward she could announce, "There is no reason why I should not make a first-grade literary reputation with poetry, which has been an obsession with me from childhood and which I have studied all my life in an effort to fit myself for such work."[44] As she wrote more and more poems, she experimented with diverse meters and boldly deviated from them when she saw reason to do so, particularly in the longer ones. To another correspondent, Mrs. Anne Pennebaker, "who found it difficult to accept the new formless poetry of the moderns," she makes the unconventional statement that "Euphorbia" "is written in the old ten- to eleven-syllable Miltonic verse form." She adds, as if inspired by Whitman, "because underlying it are the diffused rhythms of the outdoors as my ear picks them up on the highway, on the desert, in the mountains, in the meadows, in the open places. A few times it sweeps into the measures of the sea or the cañons." Later in the same letter she states that the poem's meter is "a form of blank verse as old as the hills. It is more difficult to bring out the measure and rhythm in read-ing because my ear is so finely tuned to outdoor rhythms that, no matter if I set myself a formal measure, I still find natural rhythms creeping in." She also states that "*The Fire Bird* was written in what is known as 'free verse.' It conformed to no form and measure, but ran with the winds and the waters, changing with different locations."[45] Porter felt that she had an extraordinary sensitivity to the cadences of the outdoors, a gift she shared with her father. She recalls,

> Without having delved deeply into the mechanics of poetry, my fa-ther realized that life was measured by rhythms. When he swung his ax in the forest, or his scythe in the fields, he recognized the fact that he was living poetry. He knew how the wind swept and the song of the water; he knew how to measure thought by the beating pulse of life rhythms in Nature around him. It was this thing that made him turn large parts of the Bible into poetry long before any other man I ever have known made the attempt, and he transmitted the power to interpret the rhythms of Nature to at least one of his children. I can recall climbing to the second story of the barn and sitting on a plank before an opening where I had a view of broad fields, a straight line of road, two winding brooks, and a piece of primal forest. On a beam, as on the keys of a piano, I picked out the rhythms of force and sound that I felt and heard around me and played them, even as I instinctively pick up the rhythms of the sea, of the canyon, of the desert today.[46]

In fact, Porter's poetry employs a variety of meters. *Jesus of the Emerald* exhibits a rough form of tetrameter, four clear stresses but varying num-bers of syllables, often eleven. "Field o' My Dreams" has a quite regu-lar trochaic heptameter, laden with parallelism, repetition, and catalogs, reminiscent of Whitman's work. Her debt to that poet is transparent in "Old Walt," which echoes his rhythms, lists, and epithets, such as "justly self-denominated Immortal."

Further departures from the conventional occur in some of the other longer poems, including "Euphorbia," *The Fire Bird*, and "Whitmore's Bull." They and *Jesus of the Emerald* are all consistently unrhymed. In addition, in *The Fire Bird*, Porter attempted to capture Native American sentence structure, idiom, and intonation, occasionally imitating the hypnotic rhythms of dance, and that effort also affected the cadences of the lines. Apparently fashioned for oral reading, this poem is dramatic and full of action. The anecdotal "Oh Lord,—Lady!" uses twelve and thirteen syllable lines, to comic effect.

Porter related poetry to music in a variety of ways. In some of the *Morning Face* poems and elsewhere, she attempts to transliterate birdsongs into words or sounds represented by letters. Around 1914, Porter composed a script[47] for a New York soprano named Katharine Minahan, a woman who was said to reproduce bird sounds.[48] It includes some of the *Morning Face* poems; presumably, they had been set to music. Whether such a performance ever occurred has not been substantiated, but the program was printed and includes stories performed as skits as well as the songs.

A letter suggests she had hoped to have some of her poems actually set to music. She confided to friends,

> And about the song,—this is a *deep, dark secret*, but I am not afraid to trust you, as I have before. I am not yet ready to talk, but I have written some songs I know you will like, and three of them are accepted for settings by three of our level best composers. I know you will not talk of this, I am just telling you because I think it will give you joy, and I am going to trust you with prepublication copies of the words. . . .
>
> The primitive song[49] goes to [Charles Wakefield] Cadman, who does our best wild settings, and the flower hymn to Carrie Jacobs Bond, with whose songs you are no doubt familiar, and an Irish one of which I have not a copy goes to Henry Gilbert, who has written the score for several really great operas.[50]

A search has so far failed to turn up evidence that any of these composers did indeed set a poem by Porter to music.

In structure, the poems display a concern for construction that is appropriate to their content, length, and purpose. The framework of each book suits its poem's purpose. In *Jesus of the Emerald,* the narrative of the Lentulus Legend surrounds the description of the gems. A prayer to a medicine man precedes, follows, and intertwines with the narrative of *The Fire Bird;* so, too, does a Native American myth about the way in which the cardinal acquired his red coat and black face.

Symmetry informs both long and short poems. Porter, for example, uses a series of flowers in "Blue-eyed Mary," each one for contrast to the blossom of the title. A parallel format frames the discussion of each jewel in *Jesus of the Emerald.* In *The Fire Bird,* the sequence of Yiada's three attempts on her rival's life followed by the deaths of her three children by similar causes also reflects the same passion for order.

The shorter verses show both Porter's growing awareness of conventions and her inventiveness. In shaping her poems, she rarely uses the same form twice, with the exception that four-line stanzas rhyming *abcb* recur, particularly in the captions from *Music of the Wild,* which are early efforts. Mid-career, in almost every stanza of "Peter's Flowers," she uses the rhyme pattern *abcbdefe;* in "Magic," which she probably wrote somewhat later, she employs the rhyme *aabba.* The last line of each stanza is a repetition of its first line. In the late and unusual cycle "Desire," "Fulfillment," "Apprehension," and "Abandonment," a sequence showing how the seasons mirror the emotions of four stages of life, each poem begins and ends, "I am the heart of . . . [e.g., 'desire']"; unrhymed lines of irregular length, from five to nine in number, sandwich the core of the poem, which consists of four rhyming lines.

Some poems less governed by patterns of meter or rhyme still exhibit organizational concepts. "Field o' My Dreams" follows the eye around a meadow as the narrator describes it. The narrative "The Wine of Life Pitcher" offers an explanation for the human condition, for "Life" asks "the Great Master Potter" to produce a pitcher of four parts for the wines of life suitable for "the children of good fortune," of "misfortune," of "honour," and of society's outcasts. When the Potter refuses, Life returns with a request for two cells, and finally for one, from which he will distribute equally to all infants "a universal potion, / In mixed proportions of Joy and Sorrow." What is notable (and logical) about the form is that the description of the four wines and their potential recipients is the longest, and the discussion of the universal wine is the shortest.

The language that Porter employs emphasizes how closely the prose and the poetry relate to each other. Much vocabulary carries over from the novels to the poems and from one poem to another. Favorite words reappear. "Frail," "gay," "delicate," "peeped," "wafted," "dainty," "alluring," "rare," and "exquisite" are a few that her readers will identify. She made some accommodations to the poetic line. Inversions and other combinations occur to meet metrical and other rhythmic requirements: for instance, a noun followed by an adjective, such as "poppies red," in "Peter's Flowers," or an adverb preceding a verbal, such as "swiftly speeding" and "slyly creeping" in "Field o' My Dreams." Another typical means she uses to fit meter is the contraction, as in the shift to "o'" from "of." Archaisms, including "passing throngs" and "gird" in "Euphorbia," also show up from time to time. Although the examples just cited may not reveal the poet as particularly adept or fresh with language, the vocabulary by and large remains down-to-earth and accessible. On occasion, the lines are as fresh in image as they are melodic in cadence. "Again it rolls up in sweeping curves of beauty," conveys the winding nature of mountain track in "Oh Lord,—Lady!" And, "one false step / A sprawling plunge among rocks and manzanita, / Luck if not a sheer sweep to ultimate silence" suggests the breathtaking danger of hiking along the path.

As in her prose, Gene Stratton-Porter employs figurative language lightly, but when it occurs the images are often either strikingly vivid or smoothly organic. One dramatic simile in "Whitmore's Bull" conveys the bull's power, saying that he "drove the breath from his nostrils / Like steam escaping from a power engine." Frequently, the comparisons come from nature to fit the story and setting, as in *The Fire Bird,* where "sea water . . . / Teases the pale sands of craggy beaches"; "Like the water rolling up the white sands / He was ever tireless"; and "I shrivelled like the ungathered wild plum." An image from "Whitmore's Bull" describing the night combines the unusual and the natural: "Joyous stars, like fireflies heliographing happy messages / Across the vast, rolling meadows of the sky." Rhythm and language join to convey the personality of a woman in "Oh Lord,—Lady!" in the alliterative line, "Lips having long acquaintance with life's laughing weather." In the same poem, in which the woman picks poison oak, she is tempted by the plant in the midst of "a whole world flaunting flaming invitation."

Symbolism abounds in Porter's poetry. "The Wine of Life Pitcher" represents the joy and sorrow that are part of every person's life, and the bells in "The Bells I Hear" evoke passages of human life. In the series of seasonal poems, "Desire" stands for spring and for the sexual compulsion that leads to conception, while "Fulfillment" figures both the abundance of summer fruits and the love that may characterize maturity. "Apprehension" portrays the paradoxical beauty of autumn and its omens of winter along with the concern that loneliness may accompany old age. "Abandonment" completes the cycle, the narrator facing the terrible solitude and death foreshadowed in "Apprehension," but presenting hope for spring, youth, and renewed life. Much of the poetry remains overwhelmingly concrete and literal, in keeping with Porter's attention to the details of natural phenomena.

In dialogue, the language sounds the way people really talk, including contractions and colloquialisms. One can hear the Midwestern intonations in the farmer's voice in "Whitmore's Bull" addressing the runaway and intruding subject: "You would, would you? Asked my Father." Similarly, one can hear rural Indiana in the early lines of *A Girl of the Limberlost*, in which Kate Comstock addresses her unfortunate daughter Elnora, scolding, "You've given me no peace until you've had your way about this going to school business; I've fixed you good enough, and you're ready to start. But no child of mine walks the streets of Onabasha looking like a play-actress woman" (3). The words of Billy, an orphan in the same book, might have come from the poet James Whitcomb Riley. Here, Billy responds to a question about why he isn't sleeping: "I tried. I tried awful hard 'cos I thought he wanted me to, but it ist wouldn't come" (146).

The settings of Porter's poems, like those of her prose, attest to her knowledge of and affection for the regions where she lived. Most of her books, from *The Song of the Cardinal* through *Laddie* (and several others besides those), take place in Indiana; so do a number of her poems, notably "Whitmore's Bull" and "Field o' My Dreams." "Whitmore's Bull" portrays Porter's mother's flower garden and the fields surrounding it at Hopewell Farm in LaGro County. The headnote to the poem when it was first published in *McCall's* in 1926 calls it "a marvelous tale of her [Porter's] childhood, of how the prowess and the sagacity of her father saved her mother's much-loved garden." Placing it in the context of poems that evoke Midwestern history and values, the note continues,

In such a setting, on the stretching plains of Indiana, was lived the early girlhood of Gene Stratton-Porter and here . . . she has told of it with all the accuracy of history but with all the beauty and delicacy of great poetry. She paints a picture of that far-off day that you will never forget—and she weaves into the lines a great stark tale of what life was like when all the men were valiant.[51]

"Field o' My Dreams" pictures a meadow, most likely one at Limberlost North, the site of the Gene Stratton-Porter Memorial near Rome City. The poem "The Quest for 'Three Birds'" and its twin essay "The Search for 'Three Birds'" mention a nearby location, Kestler's Island, on Sylvan Lake; and "Kestler's tamaracks," in "A Limberlost Invitation" probably refers to a stand of trees growing in a swampy area on a peninsula still visible from the house there.[52] Midwestern flowers, both cultivated and wild, abound there and in such poems as "Peter's Flowers." The poem "Blue-eyed Mary" takes its title from a native flowering grass that Porter mentions in several poems. Such idyllic descriptions of wild and domestic plants and animals characteristic of the area, frequently in the form of lengthy lists, are found as often in the poems as they are in her prose. References to changes of the seasons as they occur in the Midwest abound, as in the cycle of four poems beginning with "Desire."

Southern California provides the landscapes for two of Porter's novels, some of the magazine articles and chapters in her later nature books, and in a few of her poems, including "Ox-heart Cherries" and "Our Lord's Candles." The canyon in "Pacoima's Racing Waters" runs through Sunland, the Travers' California destination in "Euphorbia." In these writings, Porter expresses her usual enthusiasm and awe at the beauty and abundance of natural phenomena.

Gene Stratton-Porter's poetry forms a part of the seamless whole of her varied cannon. It reflects and reinforces her joy in and concern for nature expressed in her other works, her novels and nature books, her photographs and films, and even her houses and their landscaping. All of it illuminates her compassion for suffering and sympathy with human aspiration and imperfection. The poems magnify her insistence that in acknowledgment of nature's and life's gifts, one should respond to that generosity with appreciation and the exercise of one's own talents. Her "Christmas Prayer" ends with a plea for such a response, saying, "And grant a year of work and pleasure"; similarly, in "Old Walt," Porter affirms,

Happy I, content to follow, working patiently in his shadow,
Ever loving earth and sky, man and animal, with deeper devotion,
Striving to do more faithful work,
    Because of him.

Porter left a legacy of poetry that she clearly intended for her public, but it remained partly unpublished and at her untimely death never compiled. When the poems are together, their chronology shows a development from early quatrains and ditties for children to mature major works in verse, displaying a growing and astonishing range of form as well as of topic and tone. As in her prose, Porter's subjects range from descriptions of flowers and other elements of the landscape to the imitation of bells and birdsongs, meditations on the seasons, a lament for the deaths of soldiers in World War I, thoughts on the creative process, spiritual explorations, and tales of anguish, betrayal, and redemption. Her tones express wonder, humor, irony, outrage, mockery, playfulness, and affection. Much of the poetry describes Indiana scenes, rural occupations and values, the sound of Midwestern speech, and the sense of humor, drama, and perception of beauty that characterizes central North America. Her expressions of the voices and values of the rural Midwest resonate to readers both from the region and outside it. This gathering of poems attempts to honor her achievements and to make this portion of her legacy finally available.

NOTES

1. In hyphenating Stratton-Porter, I follow Porter's own practice.

2. Jeannette Porter Meehan, *The Lady of the Limberlost: The Life and Letters of Gene Stratton-Porter* (Garden City, N.Y.: Doubleday, Doran, 1928), 2–8. Most biographical information here on Porter comes from this book by Porter's daughter.

3. Gene Stratton-Porter, *Homing with the Birds* (Garden City, N.Y.: Doubleday, Page, 1919), 18.

4. Gene Stratton-Porter, "Why I Always Wear My Rose-Colored Glasses," *American Magazine* 88 (Aug. 1919): 117; also in Meehan, *Lady of the Limberlost*, 22.

5. Porter, "Rose-Colored Glasses," 117.

6. Meehan, *Lady of the Limberlost*, 19–21, 6–7.

7. Meehan, *Lady of the Limberlost*, 20–21.

8. Gene Stratton-Porter, "What My Father Meant to Me," *American Magazine* 99 (Feb. 1925): 76; and in Meehan, *Lady of the Limberlost*, 27–32.

9. Porter, "Rose-Colored Glasses," 112; see also Meehan, *Lady of the Limberlost*, 246.

10. Porter, "Rose-Colored Glasses," 117.

11. Quoted in Meehan, *Lady of the Limberlost*, 246–48.

12. Meehan, *Lady of the Limberlost*, 25, 61.

13. Quoted in Meehan, *Lady of the Limberlost,* 99–110.

14. Meehan, *Lady of the Limberlost,* 126.

15. Gene Stratton-Porter, "Choosing Words," *McCall's* 54 (Oct. 1926): 2.

16. Gene Stratton-Porter, *Morning Face* (Garden City, N.Y.: Doubleday, Page, 1916), 18.

17. Meehan, *Lady of the Limberlost,* 9.

18. Meehan, *Lady of the Limberlost,* 228.

19. Gene Stratton-Porter, "Tales You Won't Believe: The Fire Bird," *Good Housekeeping* 79 (Dec. 1924): 182–83; see also Meehan, *Lady of the Limberlost,* 227–28.

20. Quoted in Meehan, *Lady of the Limberlost,* 196.

21. Meehan, *Lady of the Limberlost,* 194, 199–200.

22. Porter, "Rose-Colored Glasses," 118. Meehan quotes two such letters in *Lady of the Limberlost,* 140–43.

23. Gene Stratton-Porter, "My Life and My Books," *Ladies' Home Journal* 23 (Sept. 1916): 13.

24. Gene Stratton-Porter, "My Work and My Critics," *The Bookman* [London] 49 (Feb. 1916): 149.

25. Porter, "Rose-Colored Glasses," 118.

26. Quoted in Meehan, *Lady of the Limberlost,* 337.

27. Gene Stratton-Porter, *Birds of the Bible* (Cincinnati, Ohio: Jennings and Graham, 1909), 69.

28. See, for example, "Hidden Treasure," *Country Life* 22 (June 15, 1912): 62; and *Tales You Won't Believe* (New York: Grosset and Dunlap, 1925), 12.

29. Gene Stratton-Porter, *Music of the Wild* (Cincinnati, Ohio: Jennings and Graham, 1910), 23–24.

30. See, for example, "How to Make a Home," *McCall's* 49 (May 1922): 2, 65; "Am I My Brother's Keeper?" *McCall's* 51 (Feb. 1924): 2, 108, 109; "Our Thanks," *McCall's* 52 (Nov. 1924): 2, 81, 82, 92.

31. See, for example, an article in *The American Patriot* by Dr. George A. Simon, "Is This an Authentic Portrait of Christ?" (Apr. 1915): 1. In her article, "Gene Stratton-Porter's Page: How I Write," *McCall's* 53 (May 1926): 2, Porter gives more details about her composition of *Jesus of the Emerald.*

32. Gene Stratton-Porter, "Having the Courage of Your Convictions," *McCall's* 51 (June 1924): 26, 28.

33. Gene Stratton-Porter, "Books for Busy People," *McCall's* 51 (Jan. 1924): 28.

34. Meehan, *Lady of the Limberlost,* 258–60.

35. Meehan, *Lady of the Limberlost,* 312.

36. Meehan, *Lady of the Limberlost,* 248.

37. Emma Lindsay-Squier, "The Lady from the Limberlost," *Los Angeles Times,* June 11, 1922.

38. Gene Stratton-Porter, "No Lazy Man Can Make a Garden," *McCall's* 49 (June 1922): 2.

39. Gene Stratton-Porter, "Gene Stratton-Porter's Page: The Healing Influence of Gardens," *McCall's* 55 (Dec. 1927): 120.

40. For example, in "Gene Stratton-Porter's Page: For the Newlyweds," *McCall's* 53 (Feb. 1926): 2, 76; and "Gene Stratton-Porter's Page: Division of Labor in the Home," *McCall's* 54 (Sept. 1927): 4.

41. Gene Stratton-Porter, "Gene Stratton-Porter's Page: Conveniences for the Cook," *McCall's* 50 (Sept. 1923): 2, 62.

42. For instance, Gene Stratton-Porter, "How to Make a Home," *McCall's* 49 (May 1922): 2.

43. Quoted in Meehan, *Lady of the Limberlost*, 247. Porter also discusses the study of poetry in "Gene Stratton-Porter's Page: Advice for Aspiring Poets," *McCall's* 54 (Mar. 1927): 142.

44. Quoted in Meehan, *Lady of the Limberlost*, 234.

45. Quoted in Meehan, *Lady of the Limberlost*, 250–51.

46. Porter, "Let Us Go Back to Poetry," *Good Housekeeping* 80 (Apr. 1925): 199.

47. Bertrand F. Richards, *Gene Stratton-Porter: A Literary Examination* (1980; repr., Decatur, Ind.: Americana Books, 1993), 72.

48. Gene Stratton-Porter, *Birds of the Limberlost, Especially Prepared for Katharine Minahan* (1914; repr., Richmond, Ind.: Igelman Printing, 1990).

49. A note on the manuscript of "Symbols," "For Cadman," indicates that she was probably referring to this poem. The other two poems are not identified.

50. Unpublished letter, "To Cochranes" (in family papers), Dec. 10, 1920.

51. "Whitmore's Bull," *McCall's* 53 (June 1926): 8.

52. An unpublished journal (in family papers) in which Porter recorded events at Limberlost North notes the slaughter of birds on Kestler's Island on Aug. 23, 1914.

Poems from
Music of the Wild

In 1910, Jennings-Graham of Cincinnati, the company that had published Gene Stratton-Porter's *Birds of the Bible* in 1909, issued *Music of the Wild*, her prose description of the woods, meadows, and swampland surrounding her Geneva, Indiana, home. Sensitively attuned to the rhythms and melodies of birds, insects, and animals, as well as to the sounds of wind and water, she divided the book into three sections: "The Chorus of the Forest," "Songs of the Fields," and "The Music of the Marsh." Inevitably, the combination of her musical ear with her reverence for the outdoors led to her vision that nature is imbued with the spiritual. Early in the first chapter, she notes,

> The forest always has been compared rightly with a place of worship. . . . Altars are everywhere, carpeted with velvet mosses, embroidered with lichens, and decorated with pale-faced flowers, the eternal symbol of purity and holiness. Its winds forced among overlapping branches sing softly as harps, roar and wail as great organs, and scream and sob as psalters and hautboys. (23–24)

Yet it is a bittersweet hymn of praise to the disappearing landscapes — the entire area threatened by oil drilling, the great hardwoods claimed by furniture makers in Grand Rapids, Michigan, the softwoods clear cut for building materials, and the swamp drained for farmland. Almost as a kind of memorial to this area, she evokes not only the sounds but the sights, odors, and changes of season in both the wilderness and tamer land.

The text is prose with photographs illustrating every few pages; there are 110 illustrations altogether. Most pictures have poetry as captions, about half by writers ranging from Anacreon to Sidney Lanier, from William Shakespeare to James Whitcomb Riley. The rest of the poems are apparently written by Porter herself. They share the vocabulary, habits such as contractions, verse forms, and childlike language and concepts (for example, the presence of fairies), that characterize her 1916 book, *Morning Face*. As there, she reproduces bird sounds. These poems, with occasional irregular meters and forced rhymes, lack the polish and skill of her later work. Nevertheless, these verses convey the overwhelming affection, reverence, and humor that she expresses for her natural subjects in all her work.

BLOOD-ROOT
It has blood in its root and a waxen white face,
Coral stems and silver leaves of wonderful grace.

THE TREE HARPS
Knee-deep in the pungent forest,
    God's Great Secret you may hear;
While to eyes of eager longing,
    The Compelling Vision shines out clear.

THE LOCUST'S FIDDLE
The locust fiddles on his shining wings,
The very same song that every bird sings,
Chants of praise for the life they know,
Notes of ten thousand years ago.

THE WHITE CLOUD
Through the forest's darkening emerald,
    In the murky, pungent gloom,
Shines a cloud of wondrous whiteness,
    Where He sets the dog-wood bloom.

MOTHS OF THE MOON

'T is Nature's greatest secret, told as a priceless boon,
In the forest I heard the night moth whispering to the moon:
"Lend thy light for my courting, if thrice in thy glory I fly,
Then from estatic loving, of joy will I gladly die."

PAPAW BLOOM

He who breathes the enchanted air,
    With eyes aflame and cheeks aglow,
Knows that earth holds no spot so fair
    As where the papaw lilies blow.

PAPAWS AND SUNSHINE

Leaf hidden are the frosty green papaws,
    In their jackets snugly rolled,
But the sun sifts down 'til he finds them,
    And mellows their hearts to gold.

BANEBERRY AND MAIDENHAIR

Baneberry white and tall maidenhair,
Mingled their leaves in the perfumed air,
Teaching a lesson worthy of thought,
For the love of God was what they taught.

A GROUND MUSICIAN

What do you think!
He tells you his name,
And it is "Che-wink."

BLACK HAW BLOOM

Winter snowballs are cold and hard,
    They often make your fingers freeze;
Summer snowballs are soft and sweet,
    And you gather them off the trees.

BLACK HAWS

As odd a thing as you ever saw
Is the changing color of the black haw.
All its berries hang china white;
Jack Frost paints them black some October night;
When the sun sees this ebon hue,
He veils it in "bloom" of silvery blue.

THE TREES

They cut them for cabins, stables and fences,
    For mauls, rakes, scoops and ladles,
They cut them for pumps, beehives and troughs,
    They even cut them for cradles.

YOUNG BATS

Fireflies flitting all around
    Wouldn't stop to be eaten;
Hungry babies too young to fly,
    Could such luck be beaten?

FROST FLOWERS

The latest snow
The Spring woods know,
Is when the dainty wild flowers blow.

THE APPLES OF MAY

The mandrake stoutly raises
    Its silken umbrella green,
To shelter pearl-white flowers,
    Apples of gold to screen.

THE SMOKE HOUSE

Through cycles the sycamore lifted its head,
    Above savage and beast with stealthy feet,
Now it stands by the old woodshed,
    And serves to cure the summer meat.

THE DESERTED CABIN
The hands that tended the cabin are still,
    Toads hop over the sagging floor,
The cricket complains on the fireless hearth,
    And weeds wave across the door,
But on blossom whitened old apple boughs
    The birds sing gayly as of yore.

HOP TREE MUSIC
Gayest music the hop trees are making,
    Deep in the heart of fairyland,
To the castanets they are shaking,
    Dance the pixie, gnome and fairy band.

FIELD DAISIES
Where the daisies march in white procession down the hill,
And the notes of the bubbling bobolink are never still.

ELECAMPANE
Its thrifty stalks thrust high their heads,
    Flowers of pale gold to flourish.
Its roots sink deeply into earth,
    Large blue-green leaves to nourish.

THE HOME OF THE HOP-TOAD
Nestled by my cabin's damp stone wall
Where wild rose petals softly fall,
Old Hop-Toad sleeps throughout the day,
But at night he's a hunter, alert and gay.

MOONSEED VINE
We plant and trim and train our vines,
Shaping them into wondrous designs;
But God's go sprawling wild and free,
Over wayside fence and tree.

MY OAT-FIELD
When the foxfire burns beside the river,
    The crickets sing under tawny leaves,
And grasshopper fiddles solemnly quiver,
    While the harvesters gather the sheaves.

BEARD-TONGUE
"There's a beard on your tongue!" laughed the lily,
    As she tossed her head with wild grace.
"Laugh all you choose!" said Penstemon,
    "There's freckles all over your face!"

MOLLY COTTON
"After lunch I wash my face
    And go to have a romp
With other little Cotton-tails
    Down in the Limberlost Swamp."

BURNING BUSH
They thought how the Lord spoke to Moses,
    When they saw its glowing flame,
And so they said to each other,
    "Burning bush" shall be its name.

TALL MEADOW RUE
Of all the roadside flowers that bloom
    The old snake fence to hide,
Tall meadow rue is the joy of June,
    Its lacy, graceful bride.

WILD SAFFRON
"Lavish my gold on the earth," cried the Lord:
    "Color the stately saffron head,
Paint the dandelion and lily cup,
    And burnish the marsh flower bed!"

GREEN PASTURES

"He maketh me to lie down in green pastures"
    Like the cattle on daisy-flecked hill,
He leadeth me gently toward Him,
    Beside the waters so still.

MOTHER ROBIN

When sleepy-time comes in Robin-town,
Four little heads covered with down,
Under the feathers of mother's breast,
Close against her heart are pressed.

THE ORCHARD MOTH

When the sun has gone to rest,
And the moon rears her shining crest,
The night moth courts in orchard glade,
To the screech owl's wavering serenade.

ROYALTY IN THE ORCHARD

The apple-tree becomes a Palace
    When the Queen-bird builds her throne,
And a doughty soldier the King-bird,
    As he stoutly guards his own.

SCARLET HAW BLOOM

The bees think the cup of the scarlet haw
The finest choir-loft they ever saw.

SCREECH OWL

The screech owl screeches when courting,
    Because it's the best he can do,
If you couldn't court without screeching,
    Why then, I guess you'd screech too.

MALE GOLDFINCH AND YOUNG

In a milkweed cradle, rocked by harvest winds,
    Hungry Goldfinch nestlings crowd and cry.
"Put seed in 'em! Put seed in 'em!"
    Sing the old birds as they fly.

MILKWEED
Proudly the milkweed lifts its head,
 And bears its pods on high,
For it lines the dainty goldfinch nest,
 And fosters a butterfly.

THE SONG OF THE LIMBERLOST
When June comes down the Limberlost,
 In her bridal garments pale,
She pauses 'neath the wild plum trees,
 To weave her wedding veil.

BROODING DOVE
We think it grief, but 't is truly love,
That finds its voice in the coo of the dove.

RED BUD
When Spring sweeps down the river,
 With the joy of passing years,
Why should the red-bud quiver,
 And weep its pink-tinted tears?

RIVER MALLOWS
The river sings its beauty,
 While the mallow leans with grace,
And softly flushes rosy
 At sight of its lovely face.

THE SONG OF THE RIVER
The river chants a triumphal song
 To the music of harping trees,
In whispers and sobs it ripples along
 To the humming of the bees.

A leaping bass flings showers of spray,
 A cardinal mounts on flaming wings,
And every voice of the summer day
 Thrills with joy of the life it sings.

GOD'S FLOWER GARDEN
Come with me and you shall know
The garden where God's flowers grow.
Come with me and you shall hear
His waters whisper songs of cheer.

THE ROAD TO THE MARSH
One misty, dreary August morning,
When the sunshine left without giving warning.

A MARSH GARDEN
They cut God's brightest flowers away,
    Dropping each swaying, graceful head,
And used the earth whereon they grew
    To make a cabbage bed.

THE MOTH OF THE MARSH
Her empty house beside her dangles,
    While her jeweled wings she tries;
Waiting a mate in perfumed tangles,
    Where the shining marsh moth flies.

UNTITLED [picture of birds at edge of marsh]
The sweetest sound marsh music sends,
    To the ears of its listening lover,
Is a long-drawn note, mellow and clear,
    The voice of the whistling plover.

A QUEEN MOTHER [picture of rail bird]
Where the Queen of all the marsh birds,
    Royal in her emerald nest,
Rules as in Venetian palace,
    On the water's shimmering breast.

THE MARSH BROOK
A sweet low song the marsh brook sings
    As it glides by Joe-Pye-Weed and thistle.

Accompanied by bees and crisp insect wings,
   And the notes of the plover's gay whistle.

THE HERALD OF DAWN
When the dawn's red glory tints the morning sky,
First the watchful Herald utters his wild cry,
Then all marsh birds answer that resounding, "Kew!"
While each tells the other, "I awakened you!"

THE FINCH COLOR SCHEME
Gold was the grape bloom, green the spray,
Nest and builder brownish gray,
Eggs and flowers pearly hue,
Master Musician indigo blue.

THE WHITE SIGN OF HOLINESS
The marshes were finished and gleaming
With crimson and purple, yellow and blue;
Then to prove them the work of the Master
He stamped the White Sign on them too.

THE HELL-DIVER
"I am a Grebe, as any one easily can see,
   But I'm badly abused,
 And my right name ain't used,
Because I'm such a deep-diver," says he.

THE MARSH ROWDY
"My heart was just completely broke
When some one went and named me 'Sheitpoke,'
So I'll roll my britches above my knees,
And romp through the marshes as I please."

WATER HYACINTHS
As the faintest murmur, at the lilies feet,
Break the rolling wavelets, in their rhythmic beat.
Heart-shaped leaves uplifted, heads of azure blue,
What the waters tell them,—if I only knew!

THE DRUM-MAJOR
He wears a modest uniform
    Of gray, with black and white,
He plays the fife till short of breath
    Then drums with all his might.
And when he can not beat his drum
    Another single note,
He fifes out, "Kerr, Kerr, Kerr," again,
    Till he almost splits his throat.

THE DRUM
On the hollow vine-girt tree
    Old red-head beats, "Tum-tum!"
Then to practice economy
    He keeps his house inside his drum.

WHERE MARSH AND FOREST MEET
Night was born in deep forest,
    In the heart of its secret place,
Slowly she creeps to the marshland,
    And veils her glowing face.

Poems from *Morning Face*

In 1916, Gene Stratton-Porter created a book of stories and poems lavishly illustrated with photographs, dedicated to a granddaughter she called "Morning Face." The present volume contains the poems and a few of the pictures from that book, *Morning Face*. Its "Publisher's Note" (probably written by Porter herself) explains,

> From the hour of this little girl's birth, Mrs. Porter improvised and recited for her amusement endless sing-song chants, rhymes, jingles, or told stories about the flowers, birds, and animals surrounding the Cabin [Limberlost North], making amusing pictures to illustrate them. When Morning Face was taken East by her parents, she missed her play-fellow and her entertainment, so once a week Mrs. Porter wrote a new story or chant for her, sending it in a letter with the illustration pasted on the back. The day came inevitably when Morning Face demanded that her stories and pictures be made into a book, then later the further request that her book be "made like the other books," so that she could give copies of it to her little relatives and playmates. So the book has been reproduced for all children.[1]

The poems in *Morning Face*, and the stories as well, have a good deal in common with her tales for children in *After the Flood* and with the poems in *Music of the Wild*. She designed the poems not only to amuse children but to educate them about natural facts, such as how ducklings behave and

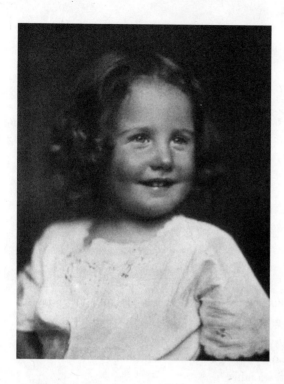

Gene Stratton-Porter's granddaughter, Jeanette Helen Monroe, "Morning Face." Courtesy of Doubleday, Page.

what birds feed their offspring. She also intended to encourage children to observe and to enjoy nature itself, matching her stated purpose in writing novels—which she described in one case as "to lead afield every human being I could influence."[2] There is a strong moralistic strain in the poems (tempered by a sense of fun), advocating obedience, kindness, love for one another, and moderation. The principal ideas, however, remain the praise of nature and appreciation of its variety.

As in the rest of her poetry, Porter used a variety of forms and meters, not always polished. Porter's sensitivity to criticism comes to the surface in the "Publisher's Note":

> When the fact was pointed out to Mrs. Porter that some of the chants were irregular in rhythm, she retorted that others were perfect, which proved that she could have made all of them so, had she chosen; but in the constant use of the names of insects, birds, animals, flowers, she would be exact, using only familiar speech; so instead of conforming the words to the metre, in the proper reading of the book, there are places where it becomes necessary to conform the metre to the words. This is the key-note of the book:

it is for the ear; to be read aloud; in many of the rhymed lines the intended and proper effect can be obtained only by chanting the lines and lengthening or shortening the syllables to fit the metre, like a rune or incantation. The book is about living things, for the most part baby creatures, for which all children have natural affection. The irregularity of rhythm, which was designed to make the lines native to children, was intentional and used for that purpose. It will require only a little practice to enable those reading to catch the rhythm, so that they will instinctively shorten or lengthen syllables to fit the metre. So chanted the book will give to all children the peculiar delight the little people of Limberlost Cabin find in it.[3]

Her actual skill becomes apparent, for example, in "The Indigo Blue Bird," where five line stanzas rhyme *abbba,* with generally anapestic tetrameter. In "The Snow Boys," trimeter alternates with tetrameter. The rhyming iambic tetrameter couplets in "Bread and Milk" seem very irregular until one realizes that each of several lines begins with a trochee (as in "Every," "Give us," and "Must have").

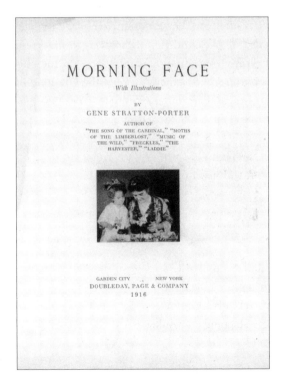

MORNING FACE

With Illustrations

BY
GENE STRATTON-PORTER

AUTHOR OF
"THE SONG OF THE CARDINAL," "MOTHS
OF THE LIMBERLOST," "MUSIC OF
THE WILD," "FRECKLES," "THE
HARVESTER," "LADDIE"

GARDEN CITY   NEW YORK
DOUBLEDAY, PAGE & COMPANY
1916

Title page of *Morning Face.* Courtesy of Doubleday, Page.

Porter often transcribed bird sounds into words, such as "Spring o' year" for larks and "Kiss her" for bobolinks. Some critics may question this device and may also disapprove of the personification or anthropomorphism that sometimes occurs in the poems; others will find such features original and suitable for children.

A childlike tone characterizes the *Morning Face* poetry. Pronunciation such as "munner" for "mother" in the poem "Rompers" reproduces that of the two- or three-year-old. "It ate the squirm" for "it ate the worm" also echoes a child's perception of the external world. Porter clearly had an ear for what children sound like and a sense of what they enjoy. This insight is as evident in the poems as it is in the novels *A Girl of the Limberlost*, *Michael O'Halloran*, and *The Keeper of the Bees*, all of which have lively youngsters as characters.

In *Morning Face*, at least one photograph accompanies each poem and story. The pictures most often illustrate the corresponding poems, showing, for example, what a horned owl or a barn owl looks like, or how a hickory moth develops. Sometimes the photos seem to provide the occasion for the poems, as with "The Unhappy Cats."

Without the *Morning Face* verses, a book of Porter's poetry would be incomplete. They show her sensitivity and adaptability to children's ears, eyes, and interests. Her sense of play and her willingness to entertain blend inextricably with her desire to teach and create interest in the outdoor world. These qualities parallel her capacity to keep the attention of the adult reader while at the same time instilling a desire to experience nature. Thus she can entertain and educate readers from childhood through maturity.

"Kestler's tamaracks" in the poem "Morning Face" refers to trees on a peninsula visible from Porter's House at Limberlost North.

MORNING FACE
When the sun scatters the shadows of night,
Until Kestler's tamaracks turn gold in its light,
When the sky is blue, and the clouds rose-pink,
When the redbird wakens the sleeping chewink,
When dew bejewels the pond lily's face,

While red waves shimmer 'neath silver foam lace,
When rainbows of light are gaily unfurled,
Then, morning has come to the rest of the world.

When its light reaches your little white bed,
Brightening sun-rav'lings that halo your head,
Touching cheeks of wild rose, eyes of sky blue,
The wondering smile that wakens with you,
Your lips line of red, the pearl of your teeth,
The pulsing white throat, the warm body beneath,
Of pain or of trouble, no faintest trace,
There, morning for me, dear, dawns on your face.

DEDICATION
One little girl with a face of morning,
A wondering smile her lips adorning,
Wishes her pictures and stories to share,
So she sends them to children, everywhere.

[UNTITLED]
Joy sailed over the morning's crest,
    Freighting a Mourning Cloak's painted wing,
Straight to its homing place in my breast,
    So my enraptured heart began to sing.

SING-SONG OF WILDFLOWER WOODS
Listen to old Screech Owl screech,
Down in his house in the big gray beech.
Mister Coon went there to dine,
And stuck his mouth with porcupine.

Swinging on a grapevine swing,
Hear old Redbird's whistle ring!
Hear him cry: "Good cheer, Good cheer!
I live in Gene's woods all the year."

Mister Rattlesnake, down in the grass,
Wouldn't let Mud Turtle pass.
Turtle bit a diamond off his back,
Guinea on the fence cried: "Rack! Pot rack!"

Old Miss Swallow wanted a drink,
Black Bass gobbled her, quick as wink.
Kingfisher watching from a dead tree,
Laughed: "Ha ha! You can beat me!"

Missus Field Mouse found a great big hole
Dug in her house by Miss Ground Mole.
"Look what you've done!" she cried in surprise.
"*Look!*" said Miss Mole. "Without any eyes?"

Ground Puppy had a crick in his back,
He went to Dr. Duck, a dreadful quack.
Duck cured the pain, but Puppy didn't thrive,
'Cause his doctor ate him alive.

Missus Pewee built her nest 'bove the door,
Red Squirrel threw her eggs on the floor.
When he ran to the closest tree,
Yellow Hammer hammered him com-plete-ly.

Mother Ground Hog stold a cabbage head,
The Paris-green made her sick in bed.
Mr. Ground Hog gave her "pod-o-phyl-lene,"
To counteract the dose of Paris-green.

Old Mr. Musk Rat left his 'dobe house,
On Gene's rarest orchid bed to browse,
Blue Jay cried: "I'm going straight to tell!"
So he rang the big dinner bell.

Gene came flying with the kitchen broom,
Musk Rat hiked back to his closest room.
If I could do just what I really wish,
I'd live there so I could help Grandad fish.

AN INVITATION

Come where the hairbell is ringing,
　Where the bluebell its worship call tolls;
Come where the Vireo preaches,
　Where the hermit his Vesper Song rolls.

BREAD AND MILK

Every morning before we eat,
My mother prays a prayer sweet.
　With folded hands and low-bowed head:
　"Give us this day our daily bread."
But I'd like tarts and ginger cakes,
Puffs and pie like grandmother makes.
　So 'smorning I said my appetite
　Must have cake, or 'twouldn't eat a bite.
Then mother said: "'Fore you get through,
You'll find just bread and milk will do."

She always lets me think things out,
But I went to the yard to pout,
　What I saw there—Upon my word!
　I'm glad I'm a girl,—not a bird!
Redbreast pulled up a slick fishworm,
To feed her child; *it ate the squirm.*
　Bee-bird came flying close to me,
　And caught a stinging honey bee.
She pushed it down her young, alive.
She must have thought him a beehive.

Old Warbler searched the twigs for slugs,
Rose Grosbeak took potato bugs.
　Missus Wren snapped up a spider,
　To feed her baby, close beside her.
Little Kingbirds began to squall,
Their mother hurried at their call.
　She choked them with dusty millers.
　Cuckoos ate hairy caterpillars.

Blue birds had worms, where I could see,
For breakfast, in their hollow tree.
   Then little Heron made me squeal,
   Beside our lake he ate an eel.
When young Screech Owl gulped a whole mouse,
I started fast for our nice house.

Right over me—for pit-tee sake,
Home flew a hawk, with a big snake!
   So 'fore my tummy got awful sick,
   I ran and kissed my mother quick,
I acted just as fine as silk
And asked polite for bread and milk.

THE INDIGO BLUE BIRD
'Cause we are Indigo Babies you'd think we are blue,
But we're gray and brown with small touches of white.
   You can see that our tummies are stuffed bursting tight,
   We flew 'way up here from our cradle all right,
And we are going to act big and sleep up here, too!

I am always a good bird and behave most polite,
   But my little Brother is one of the very worst,
   He stretches the tallest and grabs the biggest bug first,
   If he'd swallowed one more worm to-day, he'd have burst,
Mummy says he can be trusted to act a perfect fright.

I couldn't be blamed much, if I'd start family fights,
   Brother is going to be blue, but I got to stay brown.
   He always swallows the biggest, juiciest bites down,
   I think I am the one to squall, scold and frown,
I believe I'll be progressive and vote for women's rights!

THE SPIDER'S TRAP
A big black spider, homed in my tulip bed,
So that her children might be comfortably fed.
She wove her dainty web, with such cunning art,
Around every stamen in the tulips' heart,

That never a bee, called by the colours gay,
Lived to hunt honey on another fair day.

LITTLE CHICKENS

"'Oh, what little darlings!'
    We *thought* you would cry;
But will we be darlings,
    When we're fit to fry?

"From flowers you'll chase us,
    With sticks and with stones,
Then you'll soon broil us,
    And nibble our bones."

BOB WHITE AND PHOEBE BEECHER

Bob White tilled the acres of an Indiana farm,
Phoebe Beecher was his neighbour, full of youthful charm.
As Bob did his farming, Phoebe lingered near:
The birds all helped him woo her, with their notes of cheer.

"Spring o' year! Spring o' year!" larks cried overhead.
"Wet! Wet! Wet!" the gaudy flickers said.
"I'll never finish plowing!" cried the discouraged fellow.
"What a pity! What a pity!" wailed a bird with throat of yellow.

"Yankey! Yankey! Yank! Yank! Yank!" jeered a nuthatch gray.
"Hire old Sam Peabody! Old Sam Peabody!" Bob heard a sparrow say.
"T'check! T'check! T'check!" came the blackbird's pert refrain;
"Phoebe'll never have a man who's scared of a little rain."

"Cheer up! Cheer up! Cheer up, dearie!" the robins sang to Bob;
"Cheer up, dearie! Cheer up, dearie! We'll help you with the job."
"Shuck it! Shuck it! Sow it! Sow it!" advised a bird of brown;
"Plow it! Plow it! Hoe it! Hoe it! Go it! Hoe it down!"

"Bob! Bob White!" the unseen quail whistled from the clover.
"I'm plowing," answered Robert, to the saucy mocking rover.
"Phoebe! Phoebe! Phoebe!" sweet the pewee cried.
"She's coming down the lane," the happy Bob replied.

"Witchery! Witchery! Witchery!" sang a warbler gray.
"She has me worse bewitched," said Bob, "every blessed day."
"Come to me! Come to me!" intoned a woodland thrush.
"Come to me! Come to me!" Bob echoed with a blush.

"I beseech you! I beseech you!" sang a bird of golden throat.
"'I beseech you! I beseech you!'" Bob caught up the note.
"I love, I love, I love you!" the olive thrush repeated;
"'I love, I love you,' Phoebe," the joyful Bob entreated.

"Kiss her! Kiss her! Kiss her!" advised the bobolink.
Bob took his advice and kissed her quick as wink.
Chestnut Warbler warbled: "I wish, I wish to see Miss Beecher—"
"Preacher! Preacher!" cried the Vireo. "Somebody bring a preacher!"

ROMEO AND JULIET SQUIRREL
Said Romeo Squirrel: "My heart's in a whirl,
A brand new story I have for your ear.
    Let me squeeze your paw tight,
    While I whisper all night,
How fondly I love you, my Juliet dear!"

GOOD CHILDREN
Some children of the wood are gentle and good
Like you, when Christmas is near;

BAD CHILDREN
While some squall and fight, from morning 'til night,
Which should be a warning to you, dear.

THE BLUE TURTLE
Way down on the bay of Funday,
On a blue and misty Monday,
In a bed of creeping myrtle,
Hatched a scrumptious little turtle.
'Cause the weather and flowers were blue,
He always felt that colour, too.

THE HORNED OWL

"When the moonlight floods the swampland,
When the bittern's wailing croak,
And the wildcat's scream of anger
Clog the heart of forest folk,
    I search tall trees for frightened crows,
Hunt ducks 'neath sedges, hares at play,
    Then I set late travellers trembling,
By demanding until break of day:

"'Who, who, huh, whoo, who waugh?
    Don't I make cold shivers run?
Who, hun, hoo, whoo? I'd question all day,
    If my eyes could bear the sun.'"

THE BARN OWL

"When weary work horses are stabled,
When sleeping lie cattle and sheep,
    When the rat's tooth grates in the silence,
From my dark, warm tree I creep;
    I fly to white doves on the rafters,
To chickens on the stalls below,
Make my feast upon the choicest,
    Then awaken you jeering as I go:

"'Hoo, hoo, hoo, hoot! Hoo, hoo, hoo, hoot!
    Read the story in feathers white,
To-whit, to-hoot! Hoo, hoo, hoo, hoot!
    I'll call again to-morrow night.'"

THE SCREECH OWL

"When the fireflies light their lanterns,
When the locusts rasp their files,
    And the whip-poor-will's sad wailing
Fills the dusky forest aisles;
    I come from my daytime hiding,
Catch small sleeping birds to eat,

Then I cock one ear, and I wink one eye
As I give you this musical treat:

"'It's, Hoo, hoo, hoo, hoo! Hoo, hoo, hoo, hoo!
    Don't you wish you had me in reach?
Hoo, hoo, hoo, hoo! Hoo, hoo, hoo, hoo!
    Say, *how* do you like my screech?'"

A KISS
Said tulip one, to tulip two:
"There's great joy we should not miss.
Bend your tulips to my tulips,
    And that will be a kiss."

MISS CYNTHIA SAMIA
Cynthia Samia
Left her neat
Warm cocoon,
And went to try life,
By the light
Of the moon.
She met her mate
And laid her eggs,
That same night.
Alas! then
Poor Cynthia
Faded from sight.

JOHN AND JANE ALLIGATOR
Down in the land of the Cassowary,
Elephant, Lion, and Dromedary,
Close our only nice warm equator,
Lived little John and Jane Alligator.

Jane slept all day, stretched out on the sand,
John was more wakeful, toothful, and bland.
Here is the safest place they can meet you;
At the equator, they surely would eat you.

"GENE, DO SING-SONG 'BOUT THE FLOWERS"

Miss Rose Mary lost her breath,
Turned up her toes and died an awful death,
'Cos Skunk Cabbage stuck up his head,
Close beside her in the Orchid bed.

Creeping Charlie danced hop-scotch,
When he lost Solomon's Seal with his watch.
Nimble Kate tossed back her locks,
And said: "Tell your time by the Four o'clocks."

Pussy Willow went to the Milkweed bed,
To see that her kittens were properly fed.
They were scared coming home in the dark,
Because the mean old Dog Wood bark.

"Touch-me-not!" Blue-eyed Mary said,
When Sweet William tried to turn her head.
He offered Blue Bonnets and Queen Anne's Lace,
If she'd let him kiss her lovely face.

Queen of the Prairie ruling all alone,
Asked Meadow Beauty to share her throne.
Midsummer Men riding Side-saddle flower,
Came to drink Painter's Cup in Virgin's Bower.

Fox Fire started a flame in the woods,
Burned Black-eyed Susan's household goods.
She couldn't replace them for years and years,
And that was what caused so many Job's Tears.

Jack-in-the-Pulpit, smoking Indian Pipe,
Asked Joe Pye when June Berries were ripe.
Joe laughed at him saying: "I can't remember
That I ever ate May Apples in December."

Monkey Flower played such a naughty trick,
He made his Mother's Heart almost sick.

Marigold said: "I wonder if you can't
    Change his ways with Obedient Plant."

Herb St. Barbara was so very good,
She wanted Herb Robert to wear Monk's Hood.
He said: "Quaker Bonnets better suit me,
    With Moccasins, Honey Balls and Oswego Tea."

Bouncing Bet went to the Fair,
To buy Gipsy Combs for her Maiden Hair,
Lady's Thimble, Gold Slippers and Tresses,
    Jewel Flowers, Ear Drops and Everlasting dresses.

St. Andrew's Cross was heavy to bear,
When he had Dutchman's Breeches to wear.
He said he looked like the Wandering Jew,
    All dressed up in Whip-poor-Will's Shoe.

Ox-Eye winked at Adam and Eve.
Saying: "If they were parted they'd surely grieve.
I'll send them Pitcher Plant and Allspice hot,
    So they will Forget-me-not!"

THE QUEER RAIN

"I think it is very queer
But really, it is raining drops,
About as big as half a tear."

THE PATHETIC CATERPILLAR

A flock of caterpillars blue and stickery,
Lived upon my Dutch Cape hickory,
Over the beefsteak betony bed,
Among flowers yellow, maroon and red.
They had ten tan horns with tips of black,
And sharp little stickers on the back.

One, of a beauteous blue-green colour,
Was fat as any fresh fried cruller.

He looked so fierce as on leaves he'd revel,
Every one called him the Horned Hickory Devil.

He ate, and ate, with all his might,
He ate every hickory leaf in sight.
He ate and ate, oh grievous sin!
He ate, until he burst his skin.
He burst his skin, and never cried,
'Cause he knew he'd a bigger skin inside.
So when he'd burst, with resounding pop,
He'd eat again, like he couldn't stop.

All day he ate, the plump blue sinner,
As much as you'd eat for Thanksgiving dinner;
And every night, while you slept sweet,
He stayed awake, to eat and eat.
He ate until he looked greedy and mean,
He ate until his blood turned green,
He ate till he lost every skin he had;
Should he burst again, 'twould be very sad.

When he was blue, as the bluest chicory,
And the biggest 'pillar on the hickory,
A wicked green wasp observed his size,
And paused to watch him gourmandize.
The wasp licked his chops, then with his six feet,
Started where the 'pillar continued to eat.
He watched him trimming leaves like a bevel,
Then said: "I believe I'll go to the Devil."

He bit a big hole in the 'pillar's blue side,
So the greedy Horned Devil speedily died.
And when, with a loud report, he burst,
The wasp drank all his green blood he durst.
Then he cried to every wasp flying that way:
"Stop, friend, you are asked to my banquet, to-day."

The 'pillar's blue skin hung limp across a leaf,
While the rest of his family ate on in grief.
The moral is plain: Don't eat too energetic,
Or your end, like the 'pillar's, may be pathetic,
For he missed being this Moth, because of his greed,
Which is a remarkably sad thing, indeed!

KATYDID AND GALLINIPPER

Once a saucy Gallinipper
Mooning on a lady-slipper,
Flipped Miss Katydid, with his flipper,
Till she flew to the Big Dipper.

Katy sat there on the handle,
Scratched a match upon her sandal,
With it lighted up her candle
To watch Gallinipper dandle.

Cried she in a voice quite mocking:
"Gallinipper, this is shocking!
You have set my heart to rocking,
Now to you, my door I'm locking."

Pled the Gallinipper, purry:
"Katy dear, I'm in a flurry.
Don't condemn me in a hurry!
You will cause my death of worry."

Answered Katy: "Ask politely,
Prove you're feeling quite contritely,
At the slipper I'll meet you nightly,
When the moon is shining whitely."

SCREECH OWL BABIES

They just left home in the big gray beech,
And they're called Screech Owls, because they screech.

Little top owl was the first from his shell,
His parents always fed him very well.
He had sharp claws and eyes open wide,
So he was his mother's nightly pride.

Next below him comes his little brother,
Also the special joy of his mother.
His beak is sharp and keen is his eye,
He can raise your hair with his shrill cry.

Then comes little sister, neat and nice,
Instead of candy she likes whole mice.
A better Screech Owl never was seen.
She doesn't act a teeny bit mean.

Last is the baby, as you can see,
The pet and pride of the fam-i-lee,
She eats every bat that comes in reach,
And gracious me, you should hear her screech!

THE UNHAPPY CATS
We are most unhappy cats,
We don't like Mexican hats,
We don't want our pictures taken,
We feel terribly forsaken,
Want mammy and our nest in the mow,
Meow! Meow! Meow! Meow!

THE SNOW BOYS
The courting owls wake the Snow Boys white,
    When the first cold bee is humming.
So they lift pale faces to the light,
    To tell us that joy is coming.

BABES O' THE WOODS
You have a cariole, dainty and white,
With a silken comfort tucked close at night.

Babes of the Woods have a snug little nest,
And the feather cover on mother's breast.

You have a fork for your nicely cooked food,
And I hope you are never greedy or rude.
Babes of the Woods, I am forced to relate,
Must eat what their mothers re-gur-gi-tate.

THE HERMIT BIRD

In wooded tangle where vibrant air,
 With wing of down and gauze is stirred,
A miracle of pain-sweet sound burst forth,
 And lo, the voice of the Hermit Bird!

SAMMY AND SUSY SHRIKE

Sammy Shrike and Susy Shrike,
They went and fought, oh my!
Till their mother sent them both to bed
Each wearing a black eye.

ROMPERS

When I am munner's little girl,
Every hair's brushed in a curl.
I wear 'broidery an' ruffley lace,
You never saw a cleaner face;
Socks an' sashes an' butterfly bows.
I'm all sweet smelly, like a rose.

When I go to play with Gene,
Munner always starts me clean,
But she says just omperns are right,
'Cos I'm sure to come back a sight.
But I have the mostest fun,
Dressed so I can climb and run.

Gene can't bother with dry goods,
When we plant flowers in her woods.
We can't fuss with ribbons and frills,

When we go to wild strawberry hills.
We can drink from leaves of pawpaw,
But such spilly business you never saw.

We catch speckly fish in the brook,
With our hands, 'stead of a hook.
We string raspberries on a straw,
And gather apples of scarlet haw.
When I go home munner says: "It's true,
When you play with Gene, just 'omperns' will do."

THE CUCKOO CLOCK

P'raps 'twill give your nerves a shock,
But we're the *real* Cuckoo Clock.
Our first: "Cuck-ooh!" that's your warning,
To jump from bed early in the morning.
"Cuck-ooh!" at noon, plow-boy or tinner,
Hurries straight home to eat his dinner.
"Cuck-ooh!" again, sure as you're alive!
Calls you to supper, at half-past five.
When we cry "Cuck-ooh!" last time at night,
Jump into bed and shut your eyes tight.
Any other time we call "Cuck-ooh" plain,
That's a sure sign it's going to rain.

THE BAD LITTLE DUCKS

Twenty-seven small quackers, all yellow and fluffy,
Lived with their hen mother in a coop that was stuffy.
Unheeding her warnings they would run far away,
So she clucked and she scolded the whole livelong day.

She told them to eat bugs, and scratch for a living,
But she should have saved the advice she was giving.
You can see very plainly no one had taught her,
A duck can't be kept from a puddle of water.

So when thunder rolled, like a great big bass drum,
She spread her wings widely and begged them to come;

But the harder it rained the worse they amazed her.
Such things as they did completely crazed her.

They ran through the rain, and gobbled in feeding,
They quacked and they quarreled as if they'd no breeding.
The more the hen scolded the wetter they got;
Soon a big puddle formed, right in the barn lot.

Twenty-seven small ducks, each cutting an antic,
Ran straight to that puddle, which drove the hen frantic.
They swam and they dived, they drank and they gobbled,
While poor Mother Orpington jumped 'till she wobbled.

One small yellow duck gulped a nice fat snail,
Of little brown duck she could see only the tail.
The other young rascals all ate, drank, and paddled,
Until the old settin' hen went entirely addled.

She was so flustered she 'most died of fright,
For they stayed in that puddle until it was night.
Then they came waddling back, each little sinner,
With a tummy quite full of his favourite dinner.

And if you'll believe me, after acting so badly,
After scaring and grieving their mother so sadly,
She spread her yellow wings and clucked them to rest,
All the heads she could cover against her warm breast

MORNING GLORY MUSIC
We found these glories among the corn,
On a crisp, glowing September morn.
Seeds the song birds had implanted there,
    Flaunted their gay trumpets everywhere;
While many a Fairy, in robe of lace,
    To make glad music for Morning Face
Came gaily dancing over the corn,
    Each blowing a Morning Glory horn.

RUBEN AND THE REDBIRD

March

"Good Cheer!"

Ruben went to see his sweetheart, March day cool and clear,
Roadside redbird courting sang: "Good Cheer! Good Cheer!"
On the way they met their Quaker maidens gray,
All their hearts were singing, "Good cheer," all that day.

Chorus:

"Good cheer!" little sweethearts, "Good cheer," all the day,
Happy hearts and faces make a sunnier way.
Never time for pining or an hour that's drear,
While the heart is singing "Cheer! Good Cheer! Good Cheer!"

April

"Wet year!"

Once in changeful April, Ruben's steps lagged slow,
"Wet year!" sang the redbird, sweetheart's tears o'erflow.
Ruben's heart was melted, he was filled with grief,
"Wet year!" sang the redbird, for his heart's relief.

Chorus:

"Wet year!" little sweethearts, life is sometimes pain,
Hearts must stoutly battle when the day brings rain,
Sunshine in the morning, evening may be drear,
Redbird will be singing: "Year! Wet year! Wet year!"

May

"Come here!"

Then on blithesome Mayday, Ruben's arms spread wide,
"Come here!" coaxed the redbird, "come and be his bride!
Come for joy or sorrow! Come for health or pain,
Come here! Come here, sweetheart, never part again!"

Chorus:

"Come here, little sweetheart, come to love and life,
Come to him who waits you, be his happy wife,

Come on sunny Mayday, banish Autumn gloom,
Come here, come here, sweetheart, all the world's in bloom."

June

"So dear!"
"So dear!" sang the redbird, every day in June,
"So dear," sang glad Ruben, all the world in tune.
In the thicket redbird sang in trembling fear,
In a cottage Ruben, "Dear, so dear! So dear!"

Chorus:
"So dear," little sweethearts, life is joyful pain.
"So dear," in the sunshine, "So dear," in the rain,
"So dear," in the evening, or the morning clear,
"So dear," little sweethearts, always "Dear! So dear!"

July

"See here!"
"See here!" sang the redbird, wild in July glee,
"See here!" shouted Ruben, "you're ahead of me!
But next year I'll join you in a song of cheer,
When my nestling's cradled, I'll sing: 'Here! See here!'"

Chorus:
"See here!" little sweethearts, life is full and wide,
Nestlings winging, toddling footsteps, ever at your side,
"See here," little mothers, hearts of loving fear,
"See here," happy fathers, "Here! See here! See here!"

FATHER PIGEON
Father pigeon loves his wife,
    For kisses he hourly begs;
Once he crowded up so close,
    He pushed her off her eggs.

BABY FLICKERS
"They are climbing up the old dead tree,
    Every minute going quicker,

I don't want them to get away,
        But Gene says: 'Let them flicker!'"

NESTIN'
"Oh Mary, me darlin', 'tis a bright April morn,
Oh Mary, accushla, I'm so glad ye were born!"
"Oh Robin, me laddie, fair is the day,
Oh Robin, ye blarney, I like what ye say!"
        Chorus Duet
"Heigh-lo, heigh-oh, Spring ever is fine,
Heigh-ho, heigh-lo, young blood flows like wine.
There's always a bird and a tree that's too high,
While Robin and Mary are just you and I."
        Thrush Chorus
"Aeole, hiole, hilo, hilee,
Holy-a-olee, hi-oh-a-li-lee,
Oh-lee, heigh-oh-lee, a-o-lee, li, lee,
Holy, a-o-lee, li-oh-li-lee-lee!"

"Come where the bell bird and the wild dove
Are straining their throats with telling their love!"
"Sure, swate is the song-bird, fine is the flower,
I'll go with ye laddie, for one little hour."
        Chorus
"Now Mary, accushla, watch each budding tree,
And tell me, you darlin', what 'tis that you see!"
"In every tree, building 'round her own breast,
Oh Robin, me laddie, a bird weaves her nest!"
        Chorus
"Oh Mary, me darlin', in the wood love is free,
Oh come now, me sweetheart, be nestin' for me!"
"How can I, ye rascal, when trees are so high,
How can I be buildin' up twixt earth and sky?"
        Chorus
"Oh Mary, me darlin', me soul sings with glee,
Oh Mary, me darlin', I'll cut down the tree!"
"With joy like the birds, and with song like them too,
Then Robin, me laddie, I'll be nestin' for you!"
        Chorus

NOTES

1. Gene Stratton-Porter, *Morning Face* (Garden City, N.Y.: Doubleday, Page, 1916), 17–18.

2. Gene Stratton-Porter, "My Life and My Books," *Ladies' Home Journal* 23 (Sept. 1916): 13.

3. Porter, *Morning Face,* 18–19.

"A Limberlost Invitation"

"A Limberlost Invitation" was first published in *An Invitation to You and Your Folks from Jim and Some More of the Home Folks,* compiled by George Ade for the Indiana State Historical Commission (Indianapolis: Bobbs-Merrill, 1916), 7. Several versions and fragments appear in various places and forms. One occurs in an unpublished journal entry from August 1914. The third verse constitutes "An Invitation" in *Morning Face.* These versions suggest that Porter, though using a humorous tone, genuinely wanted her readers to explore and enjoy nature.

A LIMBERLOST INVITATION
Come where the chewink chewunketh,
    Come where wild grapevines swing;
Come where the craw-dads are crawling
    Over the bed of our spring.

Come where the sun in red glory
    Tops Kestler's tamaracks gray,
Come where the black bass are leaping
    And the red-wings are calling all day.

Come where the rattlesnake rattles
    While the kingfisher rattles also.
Come where the horned owl is hooting
    And it rains at the call of the crow.

Come where the harebell is ringing
    While the bluebell its worship call tolls;
Come where the vireo preaches,
    And the Hermit his vesper song rolls.

Come where the polecat's perfuming
    Mingles with flower-scented air,
Come to our swamp in its glory,
    Its joys we invite you to share.

GENE STRATTON PORTER.
Limberlost Cabin,
Rome City, Indiana, 1916.

Gene Stratton-Porter's cabin at Sylvan Lake, near Rome City, Indiana, called "Limberlost North" and "Wildflower Woods." Courtesy of Doubleday, Page.

"Peter's Flowers"

Porter's only poem on World War I, "Peter's Flowers," appeared in *Red Cross Magazine* (April 1919): 2–3, with the following headnote: "There is a tradition, old as war, that the first flower to spring from the soil of a battlefield is the red poppy. The ancient Chinese pronounced blue the 'perfect color.' All colored flower forms are supposed to have been white originally." Peter is probably an idealized composite of a number of young men Porter knew who had enlisted in the army.

PETER'S FLOWERS

I grew a wealth of poppies red, to seed the tortured fields of France;
I grew a wealth of poppies red, lest by some strange and dark mischance,
There should not spring above our lads this passion flower of old ro-
   mance—
I grew a wealth of poppies red, to sow the blood-stained fields of France.

And yet, our Peter did not like these flaming flowers of gaudy red;
He did not care for any flower that raised a brazen, bloody head.
Our Peter was a gentle soul, who loved the sheltered wildlings sweet;
He worshipped snowy violets that bloomed beneath his wandering feet.
He loved the tossing maidenhair, the trillium lily's shaft of white,
The starry campion's sheaf of lace, the creamy beard-tongue, feather
   light.

He loved the twinkling azure star, topping slim blades of blue star-grass;
He peeped in blue-eyed Mary's eyes, when loitering through her wood-
    land pass.
He loved the pure blue violets, he heard the swaying harebell's call;
The bellflower summoned him to prayer — Oh, Peter dearly loved them all!
He watched the blue flag's waving gleam, the slender aster's dainty blue;
He hailed blue sailors on his road; loved the fringed gentian's perfect hue.
He liked the shining cowslip gold, heard the adder tongue's bronze bell;
He lingered near gold celandine, and loved the stately foxglove well.
He liked all flowers of pink and mauve, and colors passing rare,
He loved the perfume of their breath, wafted on fanning summer air.

But often I heard Peter say he did not care for poppies red,
So I'll not take their seed to France to sow o'er his unheeding head.
I'd like a flower at Peter's head that's tall and straight, that's white and
    sweet,
And I'd like pixie moss and frail harebell to cover his dear feet.

For Peter, he was straight and tall; his heart was simple like a child,
Yet word was carried us from France that drove our quiet Peter wild.
His dear eyes burned a light so strange, his kind hand turned to tem-
    pered steel—
We'll take him back his Valor Cross, when by his side at last we kneel;
For we shall leave him where he lies, 'mong the brave lads with whom
    he fell;
We'll take him flowers of white and gold, and the true blue he loved so well.

And I will sow my poppies red, my wealth of flaming, bloody seed,
Where passing throngs, who read their sign, recall the Kaiser's hellish
    deed.
By crowded road, by forest path, by lonely, winding, western trail,
I'll sow my gaudy crimson flowers, lest in the coming years we fail
To keep alive within our hearts the fire that burned each gallant lad,
When he gave up his precious life, while the proud giving made him glad.

I'll sow my poppies by the sea, through sunny fields and swampy ways,
To fan the fire in us to flame, adown the lonely future days,
In memory of the lads we gave, with aching hearts, but no regret;

I'll scatter wide my poppies red, a living sign, "We'll not forget!"
And far they'll spread, 'til æon suns shall pour a pure and molten light
That fades red passion from my flowers, and turns them back to spotless
   white.

But I will sow where Peter lies, now that the last dread fight is through,
The flowers he loved of white and gold and, most of all, the perfect blue.

"Symbols"

"Symbols" was first published in *Good Housekeeping* 72 (January 1921): 12. Porter included it in her unpublished *A Collection of Poems,* and it appears in the galleys of "I Live Again." The final stanza, reproduced here, exists in manuscript, with the note "[illeg.] addition to Symbols—for Cadman." In a 1920 unpublished letter to friends, Porter indicated that she had sent three poems to different composers, including Charles Wakefield Cadman, to be set to music. Presumably this is one of them. No indication exists that any of her poems actually became a song.

SYMBOLS
Sometimes I think a pure white flower
    A holy sign must be.
Some day, mayhap I'll gather one,
    And set its mark on me.

Sometimes I think a butterfly
    A sacred symbol, bright.
Some day, mayhap I'll lure me one,
    And worship with delight.

Sometimes I think a flying bird
    Is just a soul set free.

Some day, mayhap I'll capture one
    To wing my flight for me.

[Additional stanza in Mrs. Porter's handwriting in manuscript:

Sometimes I think the woven light
    Of rainbow promise sure;
Someday, mayhap I'll stretch my hands
    Its meaning to secure.

    (illeg.) addition to Symbols — for Cadman.]

"Blue-eyed Mary"

First published in *Good Housekeeping* 72 (May 1921): 52, "Blue-eyed Mary" describes an early blooming spring wildflower. Like other poems by Porter, it expresses her delight in flowers.

BLUE-EYED MARY

When winter's chill has scarce left earth,
    And April winds blow "Hey down derry!"
Comes gaily dancing down my hill
    Sweet, laughing blue-eyed Mary.

She wears a dress of bronzy green
    Draped round her light and airy;
She lifts the loveliest face I've seen —
    Brave, tender, blue-eyed Mary.

Her eyes shine like the azure sky,
    Her step light as a fairy;
Her face, no crystal drift so white,
    Dear, steadfast, blue-eyed Mary.

My hat is off to Bouncing Bet,
    Gill-over-the-ground runs quite contrary,
Black-eyed Susan is my pet,
    But I'm in love with blue-eyed Mary.

The Fire Bird

This book had a long gestation period. Porter wrote that as a child she was well acquainted with American Indians of several tribes (Meehan, 228). Her favorite bird, the cardinal, was the subject of Porter's first book, *The Song of the Cardinal*. While doing research for *Birds of the Bible*, she read the legend of the Fire Bird bringing fire to humans stranded on the earth after a great flood. She tried to write a poem about the bird then, but it was not until some years later that she heard an illustrated lecture by Edward Curtis, the renowned photographer of American Indians, about his subjects. The next day the poem came "pouring" from her ("Tales You Won't Believe: The Fire Bird," *Good Housekeeping* 79 [December 1924]: 181–83; and *Tales You Won't Believe* [Garden City, N.Y.: Doubleday, Page, 1925]). Lavishly illustrated, this slim volume, along with *Jesus of the Emerald*, marks a milestone in Porter's career as a poet.

To
Edward Sheriff Curtis
Blood Brother to the Indians by Ceremonial
Spirit Brother to his Fellow Men by Birth

PART I
THE LOVE DANCE OF YIADA
Medicine Man, O Medicine Man,
Make for me High Magic.

Frontispiece of *The Fire Bird*.
Courtesy of Doubleday, Page;
illustration by Gordon Grant.

I, Yiada, daughter of White Wolf,
Mighty Chief of the Canawacs,
Mate of Star Face, Brave of the Mandanas,
I of your blood, I have said it!

From the roots of the white toluache lilies
Make me a strong medicine
That will drown my scorching spirit-fire
And empty my hands of their fulness.
Beat your sacred turtle drums
Loud and threateningly.
Drive back to the fear peopled forest
Of the far and dread Shadow Land
The flaming ghost of the fire bird
And the white flower of the still water.
Heal me of the dread head-sickness
Like the midsummer madness
Of foaming-mouthed quiota.

I, Yiada, proud daughter of the fierce Canawacs,
I, mate of the Brave, Star Face,
Chief of a forest of wigwams,
With ponies like the sands of the sea, have said it.
Hear me, for the healing of my sickened spirit!

Where the triumphant blue sea water,
Sky-gold all day in the slanting sunlight,
Silver-white in the uncertain moonlight,
Teases the pale sands of the craggy beaches,
Lay the lodge of my Father, White Wolf,
The savage hunter of beast and enemy,
First at the kill, Chief of great wealth,
Next in power to the high Sachem,
Chief of all Chiefs.

Many were the strong sons
Who sprang from White Wolf's loins—
I Yiada, his one daughter, pride of Falcon Eye,
His daring chieftainess, from the far Mandanas.

Tall our wigwams of deer and bear and elk skins,
Stout our warm lodges of cedar and pine tree,
Many our robes of beaver and buffalo and marten,
Heavy our necklaces with cunningly carved beads,
Polished elk teeth and eagle talons,
Shining black obsidian and precious blue shell;
Our war ponies flocking like birds fleeing winter.

Always for me, the one daughter,
The warm spot by the storm fire,
The floating sweet fat from the cooking kettles,
The first crusty brown cake
From the smoking red baking stones,
The clear flowing gold sweet
From the tall nests of the wood bees;
The soft sun coloured robe of down fine doeskin

Embroidered with broad bands of white beads,
Luring beads of green, and blue, and yellow,
The red stained singing quills of the porcupine,
And downy snow white under feathers
From the breast of the white swan.

I, first in the picking of the juicy berries
The fruits of earth and bush,
Most skilful in the weaving
Of the bright story baskets,
Swiftest at embroidering robes of doeskin
For chieftain or little fatling;
Leader in the ceremonial dances
Of the young women of our tribe,
In the great Assembly Lodge of our people.
I, of slim body, willow smooth, oak strong,
With thick long hair of crow-back blackness,
And keen far eyes like the high eagle
Of the top crag of the cloud country
Spying in the gold hunting grounds of the sun.

Many the gaily dressed young Braves
Who nightly crept close our lodges
And made soft eyes and sang wooing songs,
When the moon of full womanhood shone on me.
But always, when she braided ornaments
In my hair, for dancing,
And oiled me for high ceremonials,
In my ear Falcon Eye, my Mother, whispered:
"Keep your body for Mountain Lion,
Son of the High Sachem,
Chief of Chiefs when his father makes his journey
To the far country of the Great Spirit."

Mountain Lion was the tallest,
The strongest of our young men,
The fastest rider, the most skilful dancer,

The surest hunter among us,
The spy who never failed,
The warrior who always returned in triumph.

Like the young trees of the sea shore
He was slim and straight.
Like the water rolling up the white sands
He was ever tireless.
Like the shining of the spirit sun
He lighted all the day with gold magic;
Like the kindly silver moon
He peopled all the night with friendly shadows.
The heart of every maiden was wingéd
In the wild breast of her,
If he but looked where her footsteps led her.

Medicine Man, O Medicine Man,
Make for me a new, a sure medicine
That will ease my scorched heart
Of the fire of a flaming red bird
And take from my tortured hands
Their burden of moon white lilies.

In the cool night of the fat, bloody moon of harvest
When the tribal storehouses were full heaped
With dried fish and bear, buffalo and deer meat,
With little mountains of maize for winter;
When the cakes and candles of yellow tallow
Were moulded past numbering,
When the wide-mouthed seed baskets
Were high heaped with richness,
And many deep nut baskets were overflowing,
When the dried berries from far thickets
Made little sun painted hills —
Then all of the tribe of our hunting grounds
Bathed their hard worked bodies,
Oiled their smooth skins, painted their happy faces

And put on the wealth of their richest robes
For the Great Dance of Thanksgiving.

When the robins made love chase that season,
In the secret ceremonial of the wise old women
My Maiden's Hour had been celebrated.

Always had my proud, savage Mother
Taken me alone to the forest,
And there, beating hands and chanting,
She had carefully taught me
The Wonder Dance of the Maidens' Hour
Of the Mandanas, her people.

It was a dance of moonlight and moon madness,
Of sign love talk, of eyes asking great gifts,
Of swift feet stamping like the roebuck
And singing bead and shell trinket music,
So that all the night was softly lighted
With strange visions flower sweet.

On the day of the Thanksgiving Ceremonial
When my Mother oiled me to leaf fine smoothness,
And hung me heavy with bracelets of bone beads
And a necklace of precious carved blue shell,
As her skilled hands of love flew,
In my ear she made Canawac talk:

"To-night, before the Great Sachem
On his high throne of prideful authority,
With the son who follows him in Council,
Sitting beside his knee,
When thou leadest the Thanksgiving Dance
At the head of the young women
Thou shalt wave all of them back to their places,
And alone, before the assembled Chieftains,
Thou shalt dance the Mating Dance

Of the rich and powerful Mandanas,
Ever keeping thine eye of glad submission,
Fast on the eye of Mountain Lion.

"If the soft light in his eye strike fire for thee,
Then shalt thou forget all others
And dance out thy heart for him alone
And bow low as the young cedar before him,
And as the serpent charm him.
If he arise and stand facing thee
And dance love manifest before thee,
Then is the hour come for thy union with him.

"Then shall I fly to set up thy wigwam
Of down-fine doeskin, bleached with love,
That many suns I have worked on in hiding for thee,
And gladly in the sand before it
Thou shalt set thy lighted candle,
Thy tall proud candle of gold bear tallow;
And if he come to thee with soft words
With words of wooing magic,
Then shalt thou bury thy candle flame
In the yielding sands before him.

"Then art thou our Chieftainess in seasons to come,
And high shall thy sure heart beat
With pride of love and power,
And swift shall thy red blood run in leaping streams
With the flood-high tide of mighty Chieftains.

"Braves shall thy many straight sons be,
Great Chiefs who shall rule other far nations;
And sweet shall thy tall strong women be
As the red honey-flower that grows in the forest,
And swift shall their hearts be
As the heart of the frightened fawn
That leaps with feathered feet before the hunter."

Medicine Man, make me a sure medicine,
A strong medicine, new to our people,
That shall ease my weary eyes
Of a red bird and a white lily.

When the Harvest Ceremonial Dance
Was cried through all the village,
When night crept, silent as the bat's wing,
From the blanketed heart of the forest,
When the great Assembly Lodge
Was lighted and filled with happy faces,
When the old chiefs and the wise men
Had spoken thanksgivings for fat harvest,
And the time was come for all the tribe to rejoice,
First came the dance of the little stumbling children;
The little fat bellied round faced serious children,
With shining black hair and wonder eyes,
And flower red cheeks and mouths,
And stout breath like short gusts of North Wind.

When, worn out with swift dances,
They rolled in their soft blankets,
Came the shy youths' dance,
And the uncertain growing maidens'
All bravely tinkling little necklaces
Of squirrel and rabbit teeth, and bright rare shells.

Then danced the carefully trained young women,
Grown and ripe for the Harvest of love.
In their lead I did as my Mother had told me.

Straight I stood before the Great Sachem
And the son of the pride of his heart.
High I lifted my head like a proud pine tree,
And softly I shook my bracelets of beads
And rattled my necklace of blue shell,
And rustled the porcupine fringes

Of my fine robe of yellow,
In music like the little secret whispering
Among the dry grass under passing feet.

I spoke as I had always been taught by my Mother:
"Great Chief, grant that I dance before thee
The Woman's Love Dance of the brave Mandanas,
A dance that I have learned
From the swift feet of my Mother."

Searchingly, the Great Sachem looked at his son
And his son looked at me with understanding
And made a swift sign to his Father;
So raising his hands of authority,
The Great Sachem cried aloud:
"Yiada, daughter of Chief White Wolf,
Will dance the Woman's Dance of the Mandanas,
Let all others be seated. I have said it!"

Alone, with the blood of heart red on lip and cheek
And with the pride of my asking heart
Beating like wings on my light feet,
With my Mother keeping time for me,
As she did in the secret forest,
Slowly I stepped into the great dance
Of the Mandanas, of the peace lands;
The strongest love medicine
Ever measured by the feet of wild women.

As I danced, even as my Mother had long told me
I kept my eyes ever spying
Deep into the eyes of Mountain Lion.
When the dance grew to its swiftest wildest note,
When my proud head of certainty
And my willing arms were high lifted,
And the beads and obsidian and blue shell
Tinkled soft singing, like falling rain,

Mountain Lion sprang to his feet
And came down in the firelight before me.

With no knowledge of the dance of the Mandanas,
And no teaching of step or of posture,
He fell into the strange measures
That my Mother had taught me;
With eyes upon eyes and heart near to heart,
Facing in the wide fire flaming circle
Where envious faces kept watch upon us,
We danced the wonder dance
Of the hour of full womanhood.

Medicine Man, O Medicine Man,
Healer of the hearts of the Mandanas,
There, facing the chiefs and maidens
Of a thousand lodges of our tribe,
With the Great Sachem keenly watching
On his high throne of great power,
Darest say that was not my hour
My rightful moon of exultation?

When I looked, near the close of the dance,
Toward my Mother for guidance
She gave me the swift happy sign of birds flying;
So I caught that joyful sign
And I gave it to the waiting maidens.
Like homing swallows they swept around me;
The young Braves came stamping,
Like roebucks before the does of Spring,
Then all of us changed the dance
To the love measures of the Canawacs.

When the chattering maidens
Went back to their waiting mothers,
I stood there tall and straight and proud
Fresh as the wing of the eagle,

From the highest peak of dawn
Eye to eye, face to face with Mountain Lion.
His eyes burned deep into my eyes
With a look of quivering power.
Medicine Man, darest thou say
That was not the great understanding?

So when all of the others
Went on with the Dance of Thanksgiving,
Soft as the veiling mists
From the dim breast of evening meadows
I slipped from the Council House
And I flew to our lodge.

With hands of high satisfaction
My Mother set my wigwam beside her lodge.
I lighted my tall happy candle of bear fat;
I opened my doorway wide to the friendly moon;
Deep in the sands I set my love light to burning.
And there I waited—long and long I waited,
In burning eagerness of heart
Tremblingly listening with each breath
For the sure step of Mountain Lion.

Then, Medicine Man,
With black angered sign talk
And fierce eyes of leaping fire,
Came my storm driven Mother.
As she came toward me,
Like a killing wind uprooting the cedars,
Arose high clamour from the Council Lodge.

She caught up my hopeful waiting candle,
My living love token to Mountain Lion, my man,
She buried its flame deep in the white sands,
In rage she thrust it from her,
She snatched shut the welcoming doors
Before the eyes of anguish of my Mother
Of my willing doeskin wigwam,

And in the harsh low voiced Canawac tongue
She cried to me in choking anger:

"Woe is upon us! Strangers have reached us.
Comes a great Chief from tribes of the far North,
From the camps of the powerful Killimacs,
From the home fires of the Ice God;
And with him on a snow white pony
Rides his beautiful raven haired daughter,
A tall proud Princess of a great warlike nation.

"This night Mountain Lion will not come to thee:
His father has sent him to serve the rich strangers.
Get thee back to thy place in the Council Lodge
Before the venom tipped finger pointers miss thee,
For there will be great feasting and much talk,
The rejoicing will last for many suns and moons.
It was the wrong time for thy dance of allurement
Thy maiden proffer of prideful loving,
But I, thy Mother, taught thee thy undoing,
I, thy Mother, gave to thee the sign."

Then, Medicine Man,
As fierce a storm as ever tore the forest,
As ever pitched the sea high in wild fury,
Broke in my heart, leaping to flee its lodging place.
I lifted my head high, and proudly and silently
I stepped into the moontide,
But I trembled and shook with all-over sickness,
My blood ran hot angry gushes,
And I, who had never known pain
In any part of my strong body,
Now felt its rending arrows
Tearing my heart in sick torture,
As I crept through the restless whispering forest
Where the wise old yellow leaves
Talked over my shame with each other
And every mocking finger of night
Pointed in derision at my wounded side.

I crept back to the Council Lodge
Still as a panther fending for her cubs.
I slipped in unseen by any,
And took up my place among the young women.
On the high throne of power
Beside our Great Sachem, Storm Wind,
Sat a tall Chief trailing rich robes
Of white fox, sealskin, and white bear.
A proud Chief of savage face,
Weighted with a heavy necklace of eagles' claws,
Many elk teeth, and lion talons,
Hanging across his broad shoulders.

Standing still and straight before them,
First, I saw the stranger woman.
I heard the deep voice of her father,
Toned to soft talk, as among peace councils,
When he told the Great Sachem and Chieftains
And all the watching Canawacs:

"This is my daughter, a Princess of seven tribes,
She who can run with the foot of the hare,
Who can dance as the gold birch leaves,
When spring comes stealing from the Southland;
Who can guide the swift canoes surely
And ride the wild ponies on the chase,
Whose fingers are skilful in basket weaving,
In beading, and braiding, and polishing ornaments.
She comes with me to make the friendship
Of a people of her mother's blood;
And her name is a name held sacred
Among all the tribes at peace with us."
Like music there fell from his smooth tongue
A name well known to council wise Canawacs,
"Coüy-oüy" — a breath of sweetness —
He spoke it like the easy tongue of a lazy brook
Softly singing among the small stones of its bed.

Then every Canawac remembered the dark days
When the Great Spirit became justly angered,
And in the height of his deep wrath
Against the treachery of all tribes
Drew up the waters of destruction
Until they covered the earth's face,
Leaving upon the tallest tree
Only one Chief and his mate,
And one pair of every bird and climbing beast,
On the top of the highest mountain
Of all the earth known to man.

When the water had come up to the top branches
Until only their heads were above it,
And had stood still for three weary suns,
Then slowly it drew back, and left the earth barren,
So there was no fire to cook food
For the hungry Sachem and his mate,
Nor to warm the water soaked camping grounds.

Then the Sachem sent a beaver messenger
Far down to the underworld
To borrow only one coal
From the campfires of the dark spirits;
But the beaver was not able to bring it
For burning his mouth cruelly.

Then he sent the fierce mountain lion,
Searching all over the earth for campfires,
But there was no fire to be found,
For the water had been everywhere.

Then he sent a little gray bird to the spirit world
To bring from the campfires of the unseen country
One living coal with which to make a fire
For the cooking kettles and light-signals,
And to warm the lodges of all the tribes
That would follow him in suns to come.

So the dauntless little gray bird
Slowly winged across the far spaces.
Three suns arose and set, and at the red evening
When the third sun plunged its face in the sea,
With all of its plumage burned a flame-tongue red,
With a beak of red like hot coals
And its face blackened with fire,
Came the brave panting bird
With a living coal held fast in its mouth,
A coal snatched from the high altars
Of the far country of the spirits.

And so the fire gift was brought back to earth
To warm the hearts and the wigwams
Of every nation, for all seasons to come.

The bird was sent from a stranger tribe
Far to the south of our hunting grounds,
Where the hot suns shine and the grass withers;
But travellers journeying northward to see us,
Had told our grandfathers about it,
Had shown us the bird of bloody red beak
And face still blackened with fire,
Singing gaily in our summer forests,
Singing even in the ice of winter.

Often when we chanted songs of thanksgiving
To the Great Spirit, for rich gifts,
When we thanked him for the buffalo and beaver,
For the deer meat and fish and corn for winter,
Then our tribes made a ceremonial of glad rejoicing
For the bird that brought back
The great wonder gift of fire.

Its sacred name fell on our ears
Like the peace of the Great Spirit,
Fell soft as flying snowflakes
When first squaw winter comes,

Soft as the hunting wing of the thieving owl,
Sweet as the breath of flowers in the nesting moon,
From the lips of the Great Chief: "Coüy-oüy."

Before him, her shining head bowed,
Our people watched her in silent wonder.
She was tall, taller than any of our women,
Tall and slender like the singing wind reeds
That grow around the magic pool
Of the white spirit lily of the still water,
Far back in the valley pastures.

She moved like the night hawk
Slowly sweeping across the moon sky.
From the proud lift of her head
And the eagle look of her dark eye
From the red flower flame of her soft lips
And the sureness of her being,
I could see that the heart of her
Was like a wiry little war pony
Swiftly racing up the steep trail of her breast
With the hunt blood of the soft chase
Fevering its questing nostrils.

No woman among our people,
Had seen the beauty of her robe,
For she stood in flower white, flower fine doeskin,
Bleached and tanned like winter snowdrift,
Like the shining water flower face of far lakes,
Like the wide wing of a homing white swan,
Like the silver rays of the big cold hunting moon.

All around her feet fell soft knotted fringes
Cut deep as the height of the first upstanding
Of papooses ready to walk.
And her belt and her neck were deeply embroidered
With a thousand green stained quills
From the backs of many porcupines,

While her long heavy necklace
Was got from traders crossing far seas,
For it lay soft dull jade like the green wave meadow
In the deepest bay of the leaf tinted big sea water.

Medicine Man, O Medicine Man,
When one looked upon her searchingly,
As I looked long upon her,
That night of fat harvest thanksgiving,
Slowly one saw creeping from her bare arms,
From her firm high breasts,
Over the dark gleaming bowed head
And sure slender shoulders of her,
A faint waving cloud like fine blue mist
That could have been none other
Than the secret power of the Great Spirit,
Stealing from her breast to wrap around her
So that any evil spirit magic
Might not be strong to work against her.

I could see that she was softer
Than our hard working women,
Though she had learned from the bee
To be busy and useful,
Though she had learned from the hunted fawn
To travel far journeys in daring wingéd leaps.

PART II
COÜY-OÜY AND MOUNTAIN LION
Medicine Man, it were not enough,
Ha! it were not enough
That the stranger bore the song name
Of the fire bird our tribe worshipped;
For on her breast, sheltered with one slim hand,
With flaming wings outspread,
And panting saw-edged beak like fire,
Lay a brother of the spirit bird,
Flame red, blood red, feathers like wounds—

Dead coal black of face;
A wild thing, sheltered and unafraid.

In her language and with wave smooth sign talk
She told the Great Sachem and our chiefs
That she had found it in the forest
Wounded from the missed kill of the night bird
Or bare escaped from the eager claws
Of the hunger driven wildcat.
Even as she told how she had found it,
She folded its wings against its full breast
And set it upright on her steady finger.
Medicine Man, it moved not, it fluttered not,
Though one bleeding wing hung broken.

Where it had lain between her round breasts
Its red sign stained the front of her white robe,
The mark of her soft heart of pity.

Medicine Man, the face of the Great Sachem
Changed slowly as he watched our visitor;
He looked with understanding upon her,
He marvelled at the quiet bird.
The heart of my Father, the White Wolf,
Grew tender as he studied her.

My own heart lay strange in my tormented breast
Until swiftly she turned her face from the women
Ever the grinders of the meal in our jars,
Ever the curers of the deer meat, and salmon,
The fillers and the guardians of the storehouses;
And stretching her hand toward Mountain Lion,
By strange words and by pretty sign talk
She asked of him like coaxing birds:
"Coarse meal and water. Coü-oüy is hungry."

As a sudden wind bends a tall birch low,
Willing my man sprang to obey her bidding.

Before the approving eyes of the watching Canawacs
Never had there been a sight so fair to see,
As when, clinging trustingly to her firm finger,
The broken bird fed from her hand of pity.

I could see the deep look, the inner trouble,
The battle in the heart of Mountain Lion,
When she held the bird toward him
That it should drink, as do the wounded,
From the polished mussel shell he had brought.

He looked, not at the broken bird, as we did,
But far into the eyes of Coüy-oüy,
The Princess of the Killimacs.
Medicine Man, was it not a Brave's hour,
Was it not a Warrior's hour,
That hour in which I stood unflinching
And saw her take him from me?
I, whose heart had possessed him
Since we shot the play arrows of childhood,
And together chased the painted wings
Through the flower fields of the Canawacs.

Then came Prairie Flower,
Mate of the Great Sachem,
To lead away the mighty strangers.
For many suns and as many moons
We feasted and danced gaily.
Was I not brave to wear fine robes,
Nightly to chant boastful songs?
My breast was torn and bleeding
As the broken wing of the fire bird,
Yet many searing times
At the command of the Great Sachem
Was I made to smile in the Council Lodge,
And to dance the Love Dance of the Mandanas;
That dance that I had learned in secret

From the flying feet of my Mother,
Learned only for Mountain Lion,
For the great ceremonial of love giving.

Medicine Man, Hear me!
Not again did the eyes of Mountain Lion
Travel across the Council Lodge
To seek my eyes in understanding.
Coüy-oüy had taken his eyes;
On her face she proudly kept them,
For he saw nought but the blue mist around her,
The gleam of her hair, the red bow of her lips.
He heard nought but the luring music
Of her echo sweet voice,
And the happy song of her quilled robe
As she hourly passed among our people;
While always clinging to her breast or shoulder
Proud and fearless as in freedom,
Rode the sacred wounded bird of blood redness.

Her father homed in wigwams
Near the lodge of the Great Sachem,
Rode his hunting pony on the far chase beside him,
Sat on high in the councils of our Chieftains.

When the dancing and feasting were over
It was known through the voices of the criers
That for many moons our visitors
Would home beside our campfires,
Learning of our wisdom from us,
Teaching, where their customs differed.

The Great Sachem was swift to order,
The rarest fish from sea or river,
The juiciest of the small birds
From the snares of the children,
The tenderest fawn flesh

From the arrows of the hunters,
To be brought for the cooking kettles
Of the strangers who trusted us.

Every day I watched the slow sun,
And at night I danced with the maidens,
But no sleep came to my eyes,
No hunger came to my body.
My Mother tempted me with bits as sweet
As the Sachem had commanded for Coüy-oüy,
But my parched throat refused them in scorn,
My dry tongue found no savour in juicy fatness,
My hot hands could not place the beads evenly.

Then it was that my Mother came to my wigwam,
And closing the doorway she stood before me,
And long and long she looked far into my heart.
Deep in her eyes there gathered the black fury,
And a storm like the wildest storm
That ever twisted the cedars in wrath,
Raged in her rocking breasts
And her lightning flashing eyes.

Fiercely in the silent Canawac motion tongue,
Her look burning into my living spirit,
She made the sign of the quick kill;
And turning she slipped like a vision
From my wigwam of torture.
As she crept into the mouth of darkness,
O Medicine Man,
I knew that she had but made the outward sign
For the savage inward purpose
Long hardening in my deepest heart.

The next sun, when our mothers sent the maidens
With their baskets to the Fall nut gathering,
I kept ever close beside Coüy-oüy, my enemy,
And in my breast there flamed fierce anger,
That she had robbed my heart.

Always at the door of her wigwam,
Rocking in the sunshine of each dawning,
Hung a yellow osier basket woven like a ball,
With its ribs placed wide enough apart
To give the gifts of light and air,
Close enough to prison a flame red bird.

And there, healed of his wounds,
But forever broken for flight,
On a twig shaped and placed by Mountain Lion,
Coüy-oüy, the flame feathered voyager of air,
Sang a song filled with tears and wailing,
The cry of a broken bird heart
Pleading for wings and a mate.

The Great Spirit heard his notes of sorrow,
But I hardened my heart against the sacred bird;
For his golden cage had been cunningly wrought
By hands of such great strength that naked
They had slain the mountain lion
And taken its yellow skin for a ceremonial robe,
Its fierce name for the sign of a great deed.

Now I saw in dazed wonder
That Mountain Lion had grown papoose hearted.
He was not leading the hunters in the forest;
He was not at the head of the fishermen
Spearing and netting as of old.
He had proved his manhood in deadly combat;
He had won his name by the fiercest fight
Ever known among any of our warriors;
But now he chose to lie in his wigwam and dream,
And I knew what he dreamed, O Medicine Man!

So with soft words and pretty sign talk
I led his evil spirit to the bright late flower;
I showed her the little flitting creatures.
And when I helped her fill her basket
With sweet nuts that were greatly desired,

My ear, quick for every sound of menace,
Marked the thing the softer one did not hear.

By a slender beckoning blue flower,
I measured the distance,
And skilfully I led the other nut pickers
Far away from the spot of danger.
Then I dared her to race in turn with me
To leap the long leap across the nut bushes,
To land at the mark of the sky flower,
A fair thing to shelter death.

I set down my heaped basket of furry nuts,
I gathered my robe to my knees and raced swiftly,
I made the leap to which I challenged her,
Before her and all of the wondering maidens.
She followed my footsteps like a rift of white light.
She rose high in the air over the sweet nut bushes,
But she had not my strength, not my purpose.
My leap carried me far over the danger;
But as I turned quickly to watch her
I saw her touch earth in smiling confidence,
At the mark of the waving sky flower.

When she tore away, her eyes wide in danger,
Dragging her robe from the clinging thicket,
With greedy eyed, death hungry heart
I watched her proud face.

The Great Spirit had not pitied me,
If the curved death serpent had struck at her,
His awful fangs had missed her soft body.
O Medicine Man, make me magic for the fire bird,
Ease my spirit of the snaring water flower.

Many suns I waited in hunger and spirit searching;
Far and alone I wandered over the meadows,
Beside the white sand shore of the sea water.

One day I lost from my necklace
A carved piece of rare blue shell,
A beautiful heaven tinted shell, a treasure,
Got from traders from the Islands of the seas
Far to the south of us—across vast waters;
A big shell so precious among us that only one
Cost us the weaving of fifty blankets;
The greatest wealth known to our people.

Slipping unseen from all the others,
I went alone through a trail of deep forest
To the back of a far secret cavern I knew,
Where lay hidden my precious blue shell,
And I cut one small piece from it,
For the mending of my necklace.
When I came back to the sun, O Medicine Man,
And through the forest followed my trail,
I heard the rushing thunder footsteps
And death growl of Black Bear.

I looked, and I saw at the welcoming cavern mouth,
Hurrying in from the forest, the bloody killer,
Mother black bear, gaunt and hard chased,
With far hanging tongue and foam dripping jaws;
And behind her, panting and whimpering,
Her pair of travel worn hungry little children.

Some far tribe had driven her from her home,
And with her crying small ones following
She was seeking shelter in my treasure lodge.

I watched her turn and forbid her children to enter;
Alone, bravely to the inner recesses she went.
Her nose must have told her of my recent body,
But she could lead her sleepy cubs no farther,
For the death weariness was upon all of them.

So she came back to the cave's homing mouth,
Drove her panting cubs to the farthest wall,
And making fierce boastful war talk,
There she claimed the homing rights of the wild.

I went back to where our women were working
And I began the Brave's task of drilling my shell.
Coüy-oüy came and lay beside me, watching.
Her tribe had no knowledge
Of such rare precious ornaments.
She greatly desired to possess one
For her most precious bracelet.

When we were alone, as I worked
I told her how to find my cavern
And where the shell was hidden on a high ledge.

Her heart knew no fear;
Her eyes shone with gladness
When I told her my great secret of blue treasure
And that, if she would go alone,
She might take for herself one piece.
The one I was drilling so carefully I must use
For the mending of my rarest necklace.

When I thought of the dripping jaws
Of the killer, ravenous, tormented to frenzy,
And looked at the smoothness of her body,
I relented; I knew mercy.
It was in my softened heart
To say that the hunters must go with her;
But before my lips of compassion
Could speak the words my heart said,
With the joy light shining on her face,
She told me in happy confidence:
"I will take but one small piece
To ornament my richest bracelet,
And I will polish it smooth even as you do,
And Mountain Lion shall carve it for me."

O Medicine Man, look in mercy upon me!
Darest say she drove not her own stake,
Lighted her torture fire with fearless hands?

Darest say she knew not that Mountain Lion
Would now make her our Chieftainess?
Darest say the buzzing of a swarm of maidens
Had not told her many suns past
That Mountain Lion was my man,
That he had danced the Mating Dance
Of the Mandanas with me,
Before the assembly in the Council House
On the night of her coming among us?

All that night my eyes surrounded her wigwam.
With first dawn ray she came slipping forth
And darted down the veiled trail
That led through the deep forest.

Well had I marked the path
That ran to the cave's mouth.
When she had gone I closed the slender opening
Through which I had unceasingly watched
The moon's long journey for her,
And for the first time in many pitiless suns
I fell into the deep visionless sleep
Of the body tired past endurance.

It was near evening when my Mother wakened me.
She told me, her eyes burning deep into mine,
How hunters in the forest had found Coüy-oüy
Fleeing like a doe before the furious black killer.

When she fell, her utmost strength exhausted,
Over her raged the foaming black death.
Her beautiful breast and arms
Were forever shorn of their smoothness,
But she lived, and her hateful face of allurement
Her trouble-maker face, was untouched.

I knew what my mother knew
When she turned from my doorway.
Medicine Man, the killer had not struck
To the depth where life tented.
She had not sent my enemy to the Great Spirit.
She had only moved to compassion
The heart in the breast of Mountain Lion,
So that alone in his canoe he speared the rare fish,
Alone on the mountains he sought the tender bird,
Even the bright flower, the red leaf,
To lay at her doorway—love's offering.

Well I knew that when she was healed
He would stand tall and straight before her,
And in his fierce pleading eyes
She would find the great understanding.
Then, Medicine Man, despair settled in my heart;
I shrivelled like the ungathered wild plum,
I burned with a fierce, hot inward fire.

The day came when Coüy-oüy stood forth
Whitely robed in shining wonder,
Untouched in her courage and her beauty
Save that she hid her arms with deep fringes.

In bitterness of spirit I turned from her,
I followed the long lonely trail
Through the fringed blue flower meadows.
I lay beside the small still waters of the flat lands,
And I talked to my sister, the tall blue Heron
While she hunted food among the water flowers;
And I told the wise old Heron
For the easement of my torture,
I told her, O Medicine Man,
This same tale I tell you.

And then, Medicine Man,
The Heron gave me a sure sign.

She stalked to where a great white flower
Was resting in serene beauty,
Like a sheaf of fallen moons upon the water,
And from beneath the safety of its shelter
She picked out my little frog brother so easily.

She tossed him clear and high in the air,
And head first he shot down her long red gullet.
Then she looked at me questioningly
And awaited my understanding.

So I slipped from my robe of doeskin,
And fighting my way through the black muck,
And the snares of the entangling round leaves,
I gathered the white flower riding like a spirit canoe
That had sheltered fatness for my sister Heron.

Clean and white as storm foam I washed it,
Carefully on the home trail I carried it,
Like a living thing to my wigwam I took it,
And I put it in a cooking kettle
Overflowing cold water from mountain torrent,
Then I waited for the spirit to make me a sure sign.

That night, when Coüy-oüy's shadow touched me,
Like a star fallen from on high was her beauty.
Her eyes rested for the first time
On the white flower of the still waters.
On her knees she made a little medicine over it;
In her throat she chanted a hushed song
Of exultation and worship,
Over the wonder beauty of the white flower
That she had never known
In the far, cold land of the Killimacs.

On her face there was a veiling breath mist
Like the softest ray from the lovers' moon;
All around her wrapped the blue light blanket

That seemed to steal from her body
Creeping through her white robe.

Then, Medicine Man, I told her this fair tale:
That I loved a young Brave
Son of the mighty Eagle Feather
The Chief of a high mountain tribe far north of us,
And that when he saw me in the deep forest
Holding up high the fair water flower
The lure of its white magic
Would make in his cold heart
That strong medicine I needed,
To bring him face to face with me
In that great understanding
Which is followed by union, among our tribes.

O Medicine Man, I told her by word
And by convincing sign talk
That if her heart ran soft as gold sweetness
At the coming of any of our young Braves,
And her roving eyes flew to them
Searching for loving understanding,
Until she feared they would betray her,
And the tongue of her heart pled for them,
And her willing hands thought sweet sign talk—
If she would hold aloft the white flower,
That she had gathered from the water,
Deep in the thickness of the forest
Where none but her Brave could see it,
It would surely make for her the great magic
That would draw him straight to the flame
Of the candle she set before her wigwam.

Long and long and long again
She watched the white flower.
All her heart melted at its gold heart sweetness;
And then she looked deep into my eyes,

To spirit depths she searched me carefully,
But pride would not let me quail before her.

She knew she had barely missed
The peril of the death snake:
She had sent hunters to bring its rattles for her.
She knew she had faced the red death
By the black killer of the treasure cave;
Yet was my spirit so strong over her doubting
That once again in the chill of early morning
She set her proud feet confidently
On the forest trail I pictured for her.

She knew not how the white flower
Of the still water lifted to the sun,
She knew not the wind reeds and flute rushes.

I told her the path her feet must follow alone,
That when she saw a white flower
Like a rocking canoe cradled by soft wind,
Riding on the breast of the blue water,
She should leave her robe in the deep forest,
She should run like the chased antelope,
And leap from the sand shore
To the resting place of the flower.
She should snatch it in her hand, hold it high,
And swim back to the red beach of dawning.

But Medicine Man, O Medicine Man,
I sent her not on the meadow path
Where the war ponies fattened.
I sent her not to the still black water
Of the singing reeds and rushes,
Where the charmed spirit flowers
With sun hearts and snow faces
Spread in flocks like feeding gulls
Over the breast of the dark waters.

Medicine Man, I sent her straight to that one spot
On the sands of the great sea water in the deep bay,
In the sheltered cove of the soundless depths
Where every Canawac knew there crouched waiting
The hungry Monster of the lazy sucking sands.

Again I watched all the moon time
And in the gold red morning
She slipped from her wigwam
And entered the ancient forest.
Soft as flame ascending, swift as night bird flying,
I circled past her among my familiar tree brothers.
Long before her coming to the bay of torture,
I dropped the snaring white flower,
Fresh and lovely, a convincing decoy,
Far into the heart of the pitiless death pool
Where the eager mouths of the swallowing sands
Embrace and draw, quietly, but so surely
That no strength of arm can lift,
No power of spirit can save their victim.

Behind the rocks I hid and waited;
In anguish I prayed to the Great Spirit
That the luring white flower of wonder
Might rest on the gently heaving water
Until the time of the coming of my enemy.

As I waited with my eyes ever watching, watching
The wave cradled flower white as swan feathers,
Through the air shot the slim scarred form
Of Coüy-oüy, my hated enemy.

Her slender feet touched the water
And went down softly as a diving bird,
Her reaching hand caught the white flower surely.

She lifted her face to the face of the morning;
The beauty that shone upon her

Was like the beauty of the Great Spirit
When he had first the vision of the flower world
And the wonder of flower magic was sent to him.

Coüy-oüy held the water flower in high triumph;
She gazed at it, she laughed to it, she kissed it,
She laid it against her glad face like a papoose,
And chanted to it throaty words of lullaby.
Then with the other hand and with her quick feet
She began swimming to reach the certain shore.

When her light feet would not lift to the surface
And her strong stroke would not move her body,
Slowly the dawn light faded from her face
And a look like the look of a little hurt papoose
Came over her in slow wonder—
A look of surprise, of doubt
That her strength could be unavailing.

Then she struggled like an arrow stricken sea bird,
For the sure sands grip their captive cruelly.

Then gray terrors came sweeping upon her,
And her face was white, white as the white flower
That she held at arm's length above her.

Her black oiled braids floated out on the water,
While a cry, a shrill cry, a high screaming cry,
The voice of a wounded mountain lion,
Rang from her lips in quivering terror.

I knew who had carefully taught her
To use that cry in time of trouble:
I knew that for my Brave she was calling.
And I knew, too, how the wood and the water
Carried sound far distances to wild ears.
I wondered if Mountain Lion were on the water
Or if he were hunting the wide forest

Or if he were drilling ornaments of blue shell
Or weaving the sacred, singing fire bird
A new wigwam of gold osiers.

Only once she screamed that awful wild cry,
Then her struggles were the final battle.
Already her face of anguish was even
With the treacherous water hiding death,
Already her slender body was forever encased.

One arm slowly beat the fair bay helplessly;
But even as the gray terror closed in upon her,
The stealthy catlike death of the waves
And the little famished mouths of sand,
The slow mealy strangling sands,
She bravely held aloft the white flower.

And then, Medicine Man, I cared not if he came,
The Mountain Lion, my faithless man!
The utmost reach of his strength could not save her,
He might go down to bottomless depths with her;
He might strive and bear me down to her.
Come was my just and rightful hour of triumph!

I arose and went forth on the white shore
I smiled like a mother upon her,
Then I pointed my finger, I laughed in scorn,
I made bad sign talk at her,
I danced the Braves' triumph dance, with song,
I cried to her in the exultation of victory:
"He will not come again to you,
The faithless Mountain Lion, my man,
He who danced the sacred Mating Dance
Of the Mandanas with me in the Council Lodge,
He who read into my eyes the great understanding
Even upon the night of your coming among us.
Go thou back to the evil spirits who sent thee!"

Until the last wave overran her eyes,
The slim thing of bone hardness,
Of arrow straightness, and sureness,
Of bird swiftness, would not look once upon me,
Would not plead with me for mercy
Nor sign for help at my hands.
When she saw me she suddenly ceased to struggle,
And with her eyes fixed upon the white flower,
The fallen moon that rides the still black water,
She went to bottomless depths silently;
Slowly, slowly, Medicine Man, she sank,
Until the flower again rested
On the breast of the unconscious water.

Then I went into the forest on her trail,
I hunted her precious robe of snow white doeskin,
I rolled a heavy stone in its rich bead work:
I carried it back swiftly,
And upon the face of the white flower
Slowly sinking beneath the water I threw it.
Then I knelt in cunning like the fox,
And swiftly working my way backward,
With my steady, careful fingers
I sifted the sands over our footsteps,
Until I came to the feather grass
And the dry leaves of the deep forest.

Like the hunted I ran to the safety of my wigwam,
I buried myself in my soft robes of satisfaction,
My heart laughed in victory,
The sleep I had lost for many mocking moons
While my brain thought snares,
Now settled heavy, like sickness upon me.

Even as I slept in deep stupor,
There came dreams and yet again dreams,
But they were not familiar dreams

Of the low humming rattler
Nor the flaming mouth of the knife footed killer.
I dreamed that over my heart flamed and scorched
And burned Coüy-oüy, the little sacred red bird;
While my hands could not braid
And put the gay ornaments in my hair,
Could not put on my robe,
Could not tie my moccasins,
Could not lift food to my hungry mouth,
Because they were full of the white flowers
From the land of the still water.

When the alarum cries sounded
And the ponies' feet thundered,
When the hunting dogs raged
And shrill clamour arose in the camp,
My Mother shook me,
And long she looked deep into my eyes
And I looked into her eyes;
And then in the silent talk of our tribe
I made the swift going down sign
Of the Monster sands of the far bay.

There was no triumph on her face
When she slowly turned from me,
And fear was born in my heart
Because I clearly saw its awful image
When it sprang to life in the deeps of her eyes.

When the scouts and hunters were gathering,
When the visiting Chief was threatening,
And all of our Chiefs were in secret council,
While the women were wailing the death cry,
There came to my lodge in that hour,
The footsteps I had always awaited.
So I passed through my doorway
And in the revealing sunlight
I stood before Mountain Lion,
Terrible to face in his deep rage.

With dazed hand I drew sleep from my eyes;
I met his gaze stupidly with smiling face;
When he saw this he was forced to doubt
The thing he had come expecting to see.
When he tried to look far into my eyes for a sign
He saw only stupid Old Man Sleep sitting there
Mocking the tortured heart in his breast.

Then he caught me fiercely by the shoulders,
He drew me close to him,
He forced my eyes to meet his,
And low and hoarse he cried to me in torture:
"She jumped to the mark of the sky flower,
And the snake with death in its mouth was there;
The mark was the mark you set for her, Yiada.

"She went to the far, lonely cave
Of the chased and hungry black death,
And the rare shell that she sought
Was a part of your treasure, Yiada.

"Again she is missing, evil spirits know how long,
What torture death have you sent her seeking now—
Coüy-oüy, my brave fire bird, my woman?"

O Medicine Man, if he had not said soft words,
I might have told him as he held me before him.
I might have braved the storm of his wrath
And made my journey to the Great Spirit
In that menacing breath.
When I saw that she lived in my place
In the secret tent of his heart
I laughed at him and I cried tauntingly:
"She is chasing painted wings
In the pasture meadows of the valley.
She is at the still pool hunting the water flower:
She would use its white magic
To snare your wild heart,
Even as she used the red magic of the fire bird.

Go and seek her, O mighty hunter!
Go and seek—until you find her!"

PART III
YIADA'S FLIGHT TO THE MANDANAS
When the hunters had raced from our village
Toward the land of ice,
Toward the land of hot suns,
Toward the land of dawn,
And where the sun dives in the sea,
In the conflicting cross winds
Between the paths of their going,
On their stoutest ponies
Rode the young women and the squaws
Who could be spared with safety
From the watch of the campfires
And the care of the little happy children.

Foremost among these I rode on my fastest pony,
But to my Mother I made a secret sign
To remain in waiting by her campfire
And yet the swifter sign of the quick return.

Because I was first in the fish drying
The berry picking of earth and mountain,
The gathering of seeds of all kinds
And the work of the women,
The other maidens went where I sent them.
Then swiftly I made a wide circle
And slipped back to the lodge of my Mother,
And leaving my pony in the tented forest
I crept to the door of my Father,
Unseen by any of the watchers.

There I lay in hiding
While my mother worked silently.
She rolled a bundle of my finest robes,
My moccasins, my best bow and full quiver,

Big strips of smoked venison,
Dried fish and bear and deer meat,
Nuts and tallow cake and dried berries,
And the last little sweet meal cake
That her hands would ever make me.

When Old Man Moon made soft talk
In his canoe among the clouds,
From the back of the lodge of my Father I crept
After I had stood long and again long
Before my Mother, racked in fierce anguish,
And made her many signs of the great crossing,
For we knew that never again should I see her.

We made long straight talk between us
That when the others returned from the search
I should be missing, as was Coüy-oüy,
So that a new search would be made for my body.
Then should she cry the death wail
Through the length of all our village for me;
And make high prayer to the Great Spirit
For my safe crossing to the Happy Lands.

Thus her lodge and wigwams
And my Father and brothers
Would be saved from all suspicion of treachery,
And to the mourning of the Great Chief
Who visited our campfires in confidence,
Would be added the wailing of our tribe for Yiada.

I rode my Father's swiftest remaining pony,
I turned my face between the sun's rising
And the hot suns of the South.
I slipped through the forest and on, and on,
Each moon on, and again on,
Fast and far as the pony could run, I journeyed
In the direction where my Mother had told me
Lay the encampment of her people, the Mandanas.

When the tired pony could travel no farther
I let him feed and rest and drink;
And then again I rode, moon after moon,
Until he grew lean as deep snow gray wolf.
When I had eaten the last crumb of meal cake,
And there was nothing left in my bundle,
But tough strings of deer meat,
I came one sun-rising to signs of the Mandanas.

Then, O Medicine Man,
I slipped from the pony and bathed carefully,
I oiled my body, braided my hair with ornaments
And I put on a snow white robe
Whose bleaching had been taught my Mother
By Coüy-oüy as a secret art.
I stripped the beads and the obsidian
From my heaviest necklace for ceremonials
And wore only the sky water blue
Of the precious blue shell.

When I looked into the shining water
Above the white sands of the lake bed,
I saw in my face great beauty like high magic,
Wrought by the fear painter, the hunger moon,
The far stealthy journey, the anxious heart—
Beauty even greater than the beauty of Coüy-oüy.

And so, O Medicine Man,
At fire lighting I rode into the village.
The spies and the couriers raced before me,
Crying the wonder of my coming,
The fierce, snarling dogs yapped after me,
The frightened children ran from me,
Angered squaws with harsh voices
Cried threatening, forbidding words at me.

When I came to the door of the Council House
At the head of the long village of fatness,

I slipped from my pony, and leading him after me
I walked to the feet of the Great Chief
Sitting in solemn state on his throne;
I gave him the deeps of my troubled spirit.

My eyes slowly unfolded to his eyes
The tale of the robbed heart,
Of the tortured sleep, of the lone moon trail,
Of a fugitive from the arrows of an enemy.

With Mandan speech and by the sign language
I told him I was of his blood,
Of his tribe through my Mother;
Seeking refuge with her people,
And I told him, O Medicine Man,
These things of woe, I now tell you.

Beside him came the Great Chiefs and wise men,
Around him the warriors, the spies and hunters;
While back of the chiefs, dim in the firelight,
Again and again I felt the eye of a mighty hunter,
A young Brave, with the broad shoulders
The round face of compassion,
And the softer eye of the Mandanas
Of the lands where peace homed securely.

Little of my story had I told the Chieftain,
As straight and fearless I faced him,
Before I knew in my heart that over his head
I was speaking to the stirred heart of his son.
I was asking of him rest and meat, and tribe rights,
Even as Coüy-oüy had asked meal and water
Of Mountain Lion, instead of our women,
For the broken fire bird that rested on her breast.

As I asked I knew the answer in his heart;
For I was tall and I was seasoned,
And I was tortured beyond bearing,

And I was beautiful with a living spirit beauty
Far above that of the Mandan women around me.

When they learned that my Mother
Was of their tribe in her youth,
That I had fled as the hunted for cave rights,
They held counsel, and they set me a tall wigwam;
They gave me the rich food of a welcome guest,
And they led me to my wrinkled, gray grandfather.

The great council of Chiefs and Medicine Men,
The wise men and all of the young Braves
Made Mandan sign talk to hold me securely,
As if born of their tribe and village,
Even if Mountain Lion suspected treachery
And rode in war paint against them for vengeance.

Then was my body lazy with rich comfort
But my spirit was gray ashes
Burned out by the flames of the fire bird
Nesting in the heart of my breast.
I was all over sick for my Mother,
For my brothers and my Father, who loved me,
For the clear sky, the heavy clouds,
And the taunting water of the restless sea,
For the fat grass, the flower valleys
And the tall mountains, with head-bands of snow,
For the night fires of village and Council Lodge,
And the little honey cakes of my Mother;
While I dared not even remember
The face of Mountain Lion's agony,
As I tortured him in derision,
And he turned from me in hot anger.

As the sign was in the deep eyes of Star Face,
Son of the Great Chief, the night of my coming,
So it was in the suns that followed.
Well I knew that in the day

When he saw candle lighting in my eyes
His willing feet would dance before me
The hated Love Dance of the Mandanas.
He was a broad Brave, a fierce Brave, a warrior.
He would sit at the council in the seat of his father
When he had made his last journey
To the far Spirit Lands of final peace.
His earth-lodge would be warm
With the skins of beaver, mink and otter;
While the white dress of a great Princess
From the bleached and softened doeskin,
Beaded with the sign of the Chief's mate,
Would cover my sick heart with the robe of pride.

So hard I worked, O Medicine Man,
From the lifting to the setting of every sun,
So long I danced at night in the Assembly Lodge,
That when I walked to my wigwam
Sleep came swift and deep upon me.

Sometimes I lay visionless,
My body worn to stone heaviness;
Sometimes the flaming bird burned my breast
To gray ashes, like dead campfires,
And the white lilies overflowed my unwilling hands
Until I fought to keep from choking among them,
Even as Coüy-oüy was smothered
By the little yielding wave hidden sands.

When I had worked that season
Until the troubling mating moon
Sailed like a polished pearl canoe in the Spring sky,
When the hurrying blood of the trees
Ran fast in the red and yellow osiers,
When the birches, givers of large gifts,
Put out their little talking leaves of gold,
When strange birds made love chase in the forest
And the fish leaped high from the shallow water

As the yellow spawn they planted and quickened,
There came a night of quivering moon magic
When, after all the others had assembled,
Star Face entered the Council Lodge,
His head lifted to face the star country,
And the great wealth of his riches
Rode flauntingly from head-band to moccasins.

He had scoured his skin to fatling softness,
He had oiled his body to birch bark smoothness,
His braided hair was filled with eagle feathers,
With quill feathers of white swan
And wing pinions of wild turkey.

He was robed in the soft gray skins of the otter;
On his feet were beaded moccasins of deerskin;
In his hand was a broad fan of the wing feathers
Of the proud and contented white swan,
Round his neck lay heavy shining ornaments
Made from the teeth and the cutting claws
Of many black and brown bear,
Of fierce mountain lion and wildcat,
And the big teeth of the elk and moose,
Carved copper and cunningly pierced bone beads,
From obsidian and little singing shells.

The dance of the maidens was beginning
When he entered in high pride.
He came through the long Lodge
And stood with compelling eye before me,
And before his Father on the throne,
And his Mother, his brothers and sisters,
The whole council of Chiefs and wise men
And all the assembled people of his tribe.

Slowly he began the Mating Dance
Of the Mandana who would prevail,
While his eyes like coals from the campfire

Seared my body to action—
The eyes of black bear when he is facing the hunter,
The fierce eyes of the starving panther
When the hunger moon is shining,
The scouting eyes of the eagle of high spaces,
Seeking a mate in the far country of the stars.

When he had danced the dance of allurement
To the last stamped out measure,
Straightway I walked to the feet
Of his powerful Father, on his throne,
And in the speech of the Mandanas I said to him:
"Great Chief, thou hast seen the dance
Of thy mighty son, Star Face.
If I dance the ancient Mating Dance
Of the unconquered Mandanas
This night before thee, for Star Face,
Even as he has danced before thee, for me,
Great and powerful Chief, am I of thy people?"

The Great Chief looked into my eyes and said:
"Thou art of mine, even as Star Face is my son;
With our last arrow, with our last battle axe,
With the stoutest blood of our hearts
Will our Braves defend thee forever."

The next sun, the young women
Set me a tall prideful wigwam apart.
They bathed and oiled my heart sick body;
They beaded and feathered fine robes
For the mating ceremonials of a rich Brave.

In another tent all of the young men
Were busy preparing Star Face for our union.

Down the long wide trail
Of the swarming, bee like village
The painted criers on swift horses

Were announcing the marriage of Yiada,
Daughter of the far and friendly Canawacs,
And Star Face, the son of the Head Chief
Of the boastful Mandanas—the proud ones!

So, with the full Mandan ceremonial,
I gave my tortured body to Star Face.

There was no heart left in me, O Medicine Man,
And that Star Face might not miss it,
When he looked in my eyes in tenderness,
I gave to him such willing and sure service
As no other Chief of the Mandanas had ever known.

Soft were the skins that bedded his wigwams,
Warm his earth-lodge against the sting of winter,
Sweet was the crisp squaw bread
That bubbled in his fat kettles,
Gold was the mountain of tallow
Stacked in his storehouse for winter,
High heaped were the nuts of tree and bush
Gathered and husked against the Ice Chief,
Rich were the berries dried with sunshine,
Boiled back to tenderness, honey sweetened.

And, Medicine Man,
No other Brave served his mate as Star Face.
High and boastful was his pride
When I gave him a straight little chieftain,
And great to pain was my joy
When I oiled the little fatling:
For the fire ever burning in my heart
Had not scorched his small body,
The fulness of my hands had set no mark upon him.

He was a young chieftain of spirit magic
Who in suns before his coming to my lodge,

Had ridden on the backs of milk white fawns
Over the floating thistle seed trail
That we saw nightly in the country of the stars,
Who had played with baby beavers
In their village at the creek's mouth,
Who had hunted canyon ways,
Stout heart with bear and panther,
Who had sailed over tall mountains with the eagle,
Who had hung in the eye of the sun
With the silver winged falcon,
Who had fished angry waters with the crafty mink,
Who had raced among the white birches
With the soft eyed does of Spring,
And slept deep with his tall blue heron brothers
In their rough nests among the wailing cedars.

Every sun I watched him,
Every moon my fear-filled hand was on him.
Ever his gay cradle was light in my eye
Its tinkling shells sweet music in my ears.
When he could walk with strength
I led him to the meadows, to the forest,
And I taught him — thou knowest,
O Medicine Man, thou knowest well,
How carefully I taught him
Our every custom and tradition;
And how Star Face trained him with the bow,
To fish the rough waters, to ride the wild ponies,
And how he taught him all the laws and customs
For young Braves who would be warriors.

Thou knowest how all of the tribe shouted
When first he sat his pony alone,
And rode it through the village at its racing speed.
And then, O Medicine Man, thou knowest the day
When first he strayed far from me
With the little curious feet of childhood,

And now, now, I hear the wild shrieks of terror
When the snake that has death in its mouth
Struck its pitiless fangs into his tender flesh.

When his little blanket wrapped body,
Looking so long and straight, and lonely,
Was carried to the far, haunted death village
All the forest echoed wild cries of mourning
From a thousand wigwams of desolation
And earth-lodges that loved him.

My stiff lips made no sound,
My robbed hands lay death's captive,
For my eyes saw again the nut thicket,
And the thing the sky flower sheltered,
My ears again heard the soft buzzing menace.
Well I knew that Coüy-oüy
Had escaped the watchful Great Spirit,
That she had come back to earth
To strike me through the death snake,
That hers were the fangs of poison
Buried deep in my little fatling.

Thou knowest, Medicine Man,
How another little chief came to me,
And how again, with all the wild magic
All the wisdom of our tribe,
All the strength in our power
And the cunning of our hearts of love,
The great Star Face, and I, his strong mate,
Strove over the life of our son.

Thou knowest how he shouted
When to us there came a little sister.
And then the black day, that dread day
Thou knowest well as any,
When tall and straight he entered the forest alone
To strive for the first vision from the Great Spirit.

Without food and without sleep
I knelt silent in my lonely wigwam;
With one hand ever easing my burning breast
With the other I fought back
The slowly rising tide of the white flowers,
The luring spirit flowers of destruction
That home on the still lake waters.
I needed not the chilling death cry
That came to my ears three suns later:
I knew surely that my little chieftain
Would not come back to me from the forest.

He still breathed when the hunters
Brought before me his stout body
Ripped deep by the cruel knives of the killer.

The black death, man's height and buffalo heavy,
Lay dead in the far uptorn pitying forest
Where they had battled for their lives.
It had been the greatest fight
That youth had ever waged in our tribe.

All night the anxious Medicine Men
Made their strongest Medicine for him;
But the green sickness was eating his slender body.
In the morning, O Medicine Man,
Coüy-oüy again danced her triumph dance,
Again scored victory over me,
When our unavailing death wail
Beat against the copper face of heaven
For my little chieftain, my brave little warrior.

Because of her pointing finger no cry would I utter.
Silently in my tortured wigwam
I writhed in the flame of the fire bird
And choked with the rising sick sweetness
Of the hated water flower of the pasture lands.

But ever I held in a tight grasp
The clutching hand of little fat face,
And my ears ached with her shrill wail
For the long journey of her brother;
For she had ridden his racing pony
Before him on the saddle on far trails,
And gathered gay flowers in the valleys
On the coloured faces of high hills,
And brought me the little juicy birds
From the snares of cunning set in the valleys,
And chased the war painted wings
Where the hunting ponies pastured.
Medicine Man, O Medicine Man,
Darest say I had not killing torture?

When the burning of the fire bird was past bearing,
When the stifling cloud of the white flowers
Sickened my body to leanness,
I arose and began skin dressing and fish drying
And seed grinding and weaving blankets.

All of the squaws and the young women
Pointed taunting mischievous fingers
When, silent, I passed among them.
They said: "She is possessed of a devil;
Evil spirits drive her with secret arrows,
It is with strength stolen from the Spirits
That she works every sun at the fish drying,
The meat curing, the seed gathering
And the making of tents not needed."

But ever, when far grown I carried little Dove Eye,
Little cooing bird, on my aching shoulders,
Ever I pressed her against my burning heart:
I would not trust her to the stoutest cradle.
Tightly I held her that from my fear strong hands
She might not be pushed out by the white flowers.

When her stumbling little feet of uncertainty
Carried her to the willing knees of Star Face,
Like the first dawn of Spring long awaited
Came the light to his hungry eyes,
Like the soft talking brook water
Came the sweet words in his throat;
Like the wings of a snow white sea swallow
Writing mating signs on the blue sky of heaven
Flashed his quick hands of entreaty,
In the little love sign talk he taught her.
Many suns he sat grinding small beads of bone
Every little rare white shell he found,
And polishing squirrel and otter teeth
For the necklace she wore so proudly.

Never did I leave my hands free of her
Unless the hands of Star Face were upon her.
When he made signs of soft pale-faces
I made signs of the passing of spirits,
So he saw that my hands ever upon her
Were only that I might hold her back
From the land of the great Unseen;
For only these three, Medicine Man,
Only these three little people,
The Great Spirit sent to my lodge,
From the far land of cradle filling.

Always when we came near still or running water
I held her with the hug of black bear.
Before she might chase the little fishes,
Even in the shallow inshore water of the bays,
Or hunt the clinging mussel for food,
Or bathe with the small people,
I went before her every step
And always my feet were feeling, searching,
For any sign of the sands of treachery.
In my heart I said: "They shall not have her,

The ravenous Monster mouths,
They shall not have her, the pitiless death sands!"

Thou knowest, Medicine Man,
The season of the great pow-wow
When I was needed at the fires roasting deer meat,
When I was needed to set the forest of wigwams
For seven tribes, seeking our welcome,
When I was needed to make swift preparation,
To use all the store of my knowledge,
For the coming of a cloud of peoples
From far countries to our village,
To teach us of their experience
And to learn of our wisdom from us,
Thou knowest that day, Medicine Man—
The greatest day of the life of our nation.

I held little Dove Eye tight
Then set her on the pony of Star Face before him
That she might ride to meet the friendly people.
Thou knowest how she danced to him,
And beat her little hands in triumph,
How she snatched at the sunbeams
And fluttered her fingers to me,
Like the flying painted wings
Honey gathering over the valley pastures;
How she made me the sign of birds far flying,
When she rode away at the head of our Braves,
On the proud pony of Star Face.

Thou knowest how again and again, harshly,
I made the sign of full cradling arms,
Of tight holding, of unsleeping spying,
To Star Face as he left me.

All day the fire bird burned my heart
All day I heard his prison song;
I stopped work at the smoking baking stones,

To push back the hated water flowers
Like fulling wool from the wild sheep's back.
Ever I pleadingly prayed the Great Spirit
To have her in his safe keeping.

And thou knowest how the mighty Chiefs
Rode with bowed, sorrowing heads before me.
Thou knowest how Star Face, my man,
Stood stricken and mourning at our doorway,
His empty hands turned down in sign of torture.

Thou knowest the tale the old wise man made
Of how her glad voice chanted with the birds
And her little hands clamoured and begged,
When they passed the white flowered still pool,
The magic ornament of the valley breast,
Where first she saw the flowers of dawn growing.
Thou knowest how she whimpered,
How she reached pleading hungry hands,
How she fought to be put down to pick them.

On his pony, Star Face left her with the Braves,
While he made the welcome sign talk to the visitors,
While he spoke the brothers' friendly greeting,
While he smoked the contented peace pipe
That warmed the hearts of our visitors.
Thou knowest how she turned his war pony
And flew back over the trail, wind driven.
Thou knowest how the frightened hunters
Rode at racing speed to catch her,
And how they saw only one little hand
Not yet swallowed by the sand mouths
The living sign of coming mourning,
Tightly clutching the white flower of destruction
With its lying heart of the gold of happiness.

And thou knowest how three of our young Braves
Went down in the fierce sand mouths,

Fighting with full man strength to save her,
Until the mighty Chief, her grandfather, cried:
"It is enough. The Great Spirit has spoken.
He has taken her back to the land of short shadows.
We cannot have her. I have said it!"

Medicine Man, O Medicine Man,
Is there no magic in the toluache lily?
Is there no medicine in thy heaped storehouse,
Fat with all the harvest of field and forest,
That will quench the flaming fire bird,
That will ease its coal hot scorching?

Medicine Man, O Medicine Man,
Is there no magic granted by the Great Spirit
That will take from my tortured hands
This curse of snowy sweetness?
Call Coüy-oüy and ask if she has finished.
Tell her she has taken my all, my last little fatling,
Ask her, O Medicine Man, ask her in mercy
To send you High Magic from the Spirits,
That will empty my hands of the white flower,
That will ease from my sickened heart
The gnawing flame of the Fire Bird.

The names of the tribes used in *The Fire Bird* are fictitious. The country described
begins in the land of the Salish tribes of Alaska, runs south to the lowest extent of
British Columbia, and east to the vicinity north of North Dakota. All tribes and
country described are Alaskan or Canadian.

The End

Jesus of the Emerald

The "Afterword" to *Jesus of the Emerald* explains the origins and inspiration of the poem and Porter's religious philosophy as it had developed up to that time. In fact, in a letter she told Dr. William Lyon Phelps to "reverse it and read the 'Afterword' before you read the part concerning the subject, because I want you thoroughly to understand the why of it before you begin" (Meehan, 257).

Regarding the conception of this poem, Porter wrote in a letter to her friend Mrs. Anne Pennebaker that on the same day she had received the picture of Jesus said to have been carved on an emerald (reported in her "Afterword") she was traveling in Southern California. There, she imagined that she was "very nearly in the same geographical latitude as the Holy Land." The lovely landscape and other incidents of the day kept her from sleep that night, and she composed the entire poem before morning (Meehan, 260–62).

To fanfare of trumpet notes of ravelled gold,
Toned to timbre of aching sweet remoteness,
The prideful Emperor, Tiberius Caesar,
Shouldering wide robes of ermine-edged purple,
Entered the throne room of the Roman Senate,
Mounting the dais with court ceremonial.

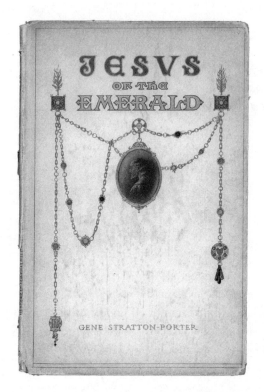

Front cover of *Jesus of the Emerald*. Courtesy of Double-day, Page.

"We have assembled to hear," cried the ruler,
"Our personal envoy, Publius Lentulus,
Make detailed report of his mission for us,
Concerning this man Jesus, of Judea;
Whose kingly aspirations letters to us
From Pontius Pilate, ruling this province,
Give our august body full information.
We should be at pains to be informed about
This offspring of a Virgin, of Bethlehem;
This fatherless son, a carpenter fosters;
This daily worker of mighty miracles;
This healer of the deformed and bed-ridden,
Whom a deluded host leaves flocks and vineyards
To follow, gaping, in spellbound multitudes."

Lentulus, the Envoy, bowed before Caesar
And thus detailed his mission to Palestine:

"Hail, mighty Emperor! Hail, wise Senators!
Three days did I follow in each footstep,
Hearing the words and watching the saving works
Of this strange man of Nazareth, called Jesus
By the exulting hosts who follow his path.
He is a man of stature, tall and comely,
Wearing a very reverend countenance
Such as the beholder must both love and fear.
His hair is the colour of a ripe chestnut,
Plain to the ears, hence downward more orient,
Curling and waving over the broad shoulders.
Set in the very midst of his high forehead
There is a stream, or partition, in his hair,
After the manner of all good Nazarites.
His forehead is plain and very delicate,
His face unblemished, without spot or wrinkle,
And beautiful with a lovely red colour,
His nose and mouth so marked as words fail to tell.
His short beard is thick, in colour like his hair,
His look is mature, but purely innocent.
His full, far-seeing eyes are gray, quick and clear.
In reproof he is terrible to behold;
In admonishing, of courteous, fair speech;
Pleasant in conversation, grave of habit.
I had speech with no one who had seen him laugh;
Many had seen him weep tears of compassion.
His proportion of body is excellent;
His kind hands and arms, delightful to behold."

Slowly the look of prideful security
Faded from the face of the great Emperor.
"Now give us thy conclusions concerning him,
O Lentulus, our Envoy," he commanded.

In measured words Lentulus thus made answer:
"O King! This man Jesus wears God-like beauty;
A powerful leader, his strength enduring,
He treads deep valleys and rough hill passes.

He preaches the long promised coming of Christ
To the workers in the fields and villages,
And with sufficient hands of indignation,
Alone, drives the usurers from the temple.
He travels the length of the Jordan on foot;
He gathers a multitude beside the seas;
No temple will house the hosts who follow him.
He exalts the lowly, he humbles the proud;
He comforts the sad, he heals the sick body;
At his touch the lame walk, the dead are restored—"

"Saw you these marvels?" cried Caesar in wonder,
His face mist white, his hands of power trembling.

Slowly made answer the Envoy, Lentulus:
"Of a verity, mine eyes saw them, O King!
His voice stills the tempest on wild Galilee;
His hand changes water to heartening wine;
Weavers forsake their looms, shepherds their own flocks,
Rich men bring their wealth to him to distribute;
The poor yield the greater riches of service.
Awed thousands follow him throughout the whole day,
And sleep near him on the hospitable earth,
Feasting on a few loaves and little fishes
That with his hands of dazing accomplishment
He breaks into baskets heaped high with plenty
In the sight of numberless, worshipping hosts.
I marvel that all Judea obeys him."

"Have done, wise and just Lentulus!" cried Caesar.

With bowed head and bitter heart the Emperor
Arose in haste and left the Senate Chamber,
His heart shaken with jealous apprehension.
Reports had crossed the sea, of a wise Healer,
A man speaking with the surety of Prophets;
But in his troubled heart, Caesar feared a king.
From the words of Lentulus to the Senate,
The Emperor visioned a powerful man,

More comely than any god of Greece or Rome,
Gathering a vast multitude around him
With the magic of words of loving-kindness;
But in Caesar's mind the host so assembled
Wore shields and carried the swords and spears of war,
While with compelling force they swept due westward,
Their faces set toward the seven hills of Rome.

Within the same hour the Emperor summoned
The Master Craftsman of his entire kingdom:
"Go thou to the land of Judea," he said.
"Follow the footsteps, study well the person
Of this man, Jesus, who is arousing hosts,
Until you can draw for me his true likeness."

Then Caesar, ambitious of world dominion,
Brooded by day and muttered in his slumber,
Until the return of the Master Artist.

Carefully the Craftsman drew from his bosom
A well protected drawing on fine parchment,
Fearfully yielding it to the eager hands
Outstretched by the inexorable Ruler.

"Like that? Not like that!" cried Caesar in wonder.

"Like that, your Majesty," said the great Artist.
"Many days I walked with Jesus, hearing Him.
His chosen Disciples call Him a Healer;
Among his converts are men speaking freely,
Speaking openly of forming a kingdom;
And some there be who whisper to each other
That this worker of miracles is the Christ."

The parchment shook in the hands of the ruler.
His startled eyes were searching, deeply searching;
Then with circumspection, he leaned to whisper:
"With this face, in truth, He might be! — He might be!"

To the Master Craftsman came his quick command:
"Such arresting beauty should be enduring.
I will not risk the mercy of gorging flames
Or wind malice, be He Prophet, King or Christ.
Get you to my treasure vaults with their keeper.
From my living jewels choose that stone you will;
Not one will prove of sufficient excellence;
Then grave this likeness exactly upon it."

Long the Master Craftsman thoughtfully studied
Stones that had ransomed the heads of great kings,
Proud jewels that made up the richest treasure
Brought to Rome by victorious argosies.

Deeply he studied the translucent white wealth,
Iridescent as bubbles afloat in the sun.
He saw God in the rainbow, arching the sky,
The modest lilies of peaceful, dim valleys,
And heard the cooed mating notes of white doves,
Nesting deep in the beneficent olives.
He visioned the wide wings of the snowy stork
Trailing homing shadows across Italy,
The alabaster ledges of white Carrara,
And the ice mantle and heavy snow blanket
Draping the shoulders of grim Alpine giants.
Slowly he pushed aside the lure of whiteness:
His brain sought not the emblem of purity.

Meditatively he touched the gold topaz.
It seemed that the yellow lilies of the field
Were deeply mirrored in its clear remoteness.
He saw the faithful, amber-feathered hoopoe
Winging life to his walled-in mate and nestlings,
And heard the golden plover drumming love notes
On each thickly wooded hill of Tuscany.
In this jewel's depths he visioned the orange fruit
And all the creeping gold of lavish nature.
He saw the treasure of molten sun-like wealth,

Deeply buried in the pulsing heart of earth;
The life giving rays of the light of the world
Jealously held fast in its shining compass.
But he could not feel the symbol of riches
To be the stone that his moved heart demanded
On which to set forever the God-like face
Of the man he had learned on his strange journey
To believe to be the long promised Saviour.

Then flashed the multiple lure of the sapphire.
He saw blue violets on the far hills of Parma,
Mingling the passion of their luring sweet breath
With the contrary winds of light adventure.
He saw the migrant blue wings of happiness
Sweeping the sky toward the gardens of Gaul;
Visioned the perfect blue of truth, enduring,
Roofing the world with its sparkling splendour,
Mirrored in the unstable waters of earth.
But he sought more than symbols of truth or joy
In the stone chosen for his loved commission.

Longer he pondered the blood of the ruby.
He remembered its flaming symbol in Spring
Decorating the boughs of the pomegranate,
On the burning wings of the jealous macaw,
Screaming among the palms in the courts of kings.
In the beading heart of this stone he could see
The swift red streams of pulsing human passion,
The mouth of the war dragon, dripping hot blood,
The wrath of Vesuvius, belching in anger,
A pool of life wine — the emblem of earth love,
But not symbolic of the redeeming love
Manifest in the heart of the Nazarene.

He held to light a great, flawless emerald,
The price of the head of a prince of Persia;
And gazing deep in its heart of allurement,
Saw the green of annual resurrection

Waking to life every hillside of the world.
He saw the fig tree put forth its tender leaf,
The almond reclothe its boughs in fresh beauty,
The grape's lavish promise of enduring cheer.
Saw every forest girdling the far earth's face,
Hourly rejoicing in low, singing wonder.
Saw the still mosses spread their gentle velvet
In mercy, covering earth's signs of decay.
He watched the valiant, warring blades of grass
Carrying on their conquest of waste places;
Marching down highways in joyous adventure,
Grateful to the teeth of the grazing cattle.
He saw the hopeful green reward the sower,
The feathered precursors of lilies waving.
He peered into remote depths of the ocean,
And among the verdant orchards of the sea,
Found emerald fishes, shells of abalone.
He watched the gay wood duck float the still water,
He saw the glittering peacock flout the sun.
He heard the leaf-green parrots' raucous crying,
The cuddling love birds whispering endearments.
To the custodian of the vaults he said:
"This is the jewel I take in my keeping
For the execution of my commission;
For this is the symbol in stone that is living,
Typifying the resurrection of life."

Back to the tools littering his work table
Hastened the feet of the great Master Craftsman.
Scarcely he ventured to draw the breath of life
To life sustaining depth and hearty volume
Fearing for the sureness of his cunning hand.

One line of grace from forehead to curve of chin
Must surely set the world's most perfect profile.
To trace the mouth of sensitive compassion
His utmost skill, that day, he gravely doubted.

With prayer he studied his revered drawing,
All his soul pleading for high inspiration.
And then his heart heard a voice of redemption
That drifted from the white sands of Galilee:
"Our Father, which art in Heaven—forgive us"
"Suffer little children, and forbid them not"
"I am not sent but unto the earth's lost sheep"
"Come, ye who are weary and heavy laden"
"Blessed are the merciful—they shall know mercy"
"Thou shalt love the Lord, thy God, with all thy heart"
"Be of good cheer. It is I. Be not afraid!"
"Cast thy bread upon the waters—it shall return"
"Thou shalt love thy neighbour even as thyself"
"All things whatsoever ye would—do ye even so"
"Lay not up for yourselves treasures on earth"
"Render—to Caesar the things which are Caesar's"
To all our beloved dead: "Arise, and come forth."
To the uncertain blind: "Look up and see."
To the lame: "Arise, take up thy bed and walk."
To the loathsome leper: "I will; be thou clean."
To Galilee's mad waters: "Peace, be still!"

With certitude the Master could carve them then,
Proud lips that spoke free, triumphant salvation.
Ultimate hope for a bewildered world.
One sweep of beauty for the line of the chin,
The perfect brow, a slender, serene bow,
And that eye, surely piercing hypocrisy,
That quick eye that could unfailingly penetrate
Where blackest shadows lay in the hearts of men.
Then the column of the throat of a strong man—
The outdoor man, of far highway and rough sea,
Frequenting the temple of Jerusalem,
Homing in small, star-arresting Bethlehem,
Where singing worlds paused in coursing the heavens
To show other worlds where a God had been born—
But it must be pulsing! Vibrantly pulsing!

Its hollow must throb, even on stone, must throb
With the deep throes of a heart of compassion,
Weighted with the burthen of a sinning world.

Then the Master reproduced in full detail
Each wave of beauty of the dark chestnut hair,
Of the short, heavy beard, brightly undulant,
The many folds of the enveloping mantle.
So the sacred commission was finished;
Upon enduring stone was set forever
The only true likeness of the living God,
    Jesus Christ, of the emerald.

AFTERWORD

During the seven years prior to 1909, while collecting material from the treasures of the world of books and art for a work concerning the birds of the Bible, I found what is known to students of ancient history as the "Lentulus Legend" concerning the personal appearance and the work of Jesus Christ. This description so agreed with my conception of the person of Jesus Christ that I used it in my book, taking especial care to state that the material was submitted to the Roman senate by Publius Lentulus, a personal envoy of Tiberius Caesar, since history does not support the sometime assumption that he was a Roman senator. Some have thought that Lentulus was the predecessor of Pilate as governor of Judea, holding office under Herod, the king. In the historical work of Flavius Josephus, entitled "Antiquities of the Jews," Book Fourteen, Chapter Ten, Page 386, Paragraph Four, there is a mention of a Publius Lentulus who was the father of Lucius Lentulus, a consul, who was extremely active in securing an increase of pay for the army, so that his father might have been a consul also, and especially available as the personal envoy of Tiberius.

A great many historians are of the opinion that Flavius Josephus was a painstaking and accurate historian and that his records are correct. Contradicting this are the following authorities who disagree with him:

In the "Dictionary of Greek and Roman Biography and Mythology" by Smith, Volume Two, Page 729, there is given a list of the members of the Lentulus family, but in this list Publius Lentulus is described as having taken part in the Conspiracy of Catiline which was sixty-three years before the birth of Christ. There is a Cossus Cornelius Lentulus who was consul in the year One before Christ. On the accession of Tiberius Caesar fourteen years after Christ, he accompanied Drusus to Pomonia to quell a mutiny. In A.D. 16 he took part in a debate in the senate respecting Libo and in A.D. 22 respecting Silanus, and again in A.D. 24, when he was accused of majestos. He died A.D. 25 leaving behind him an honourable reputation. His son became consul A.D. 26. He was a writer and Tiberius Caesar was thought to have been afraid of him because of his large influence with the army. He is also mentioned in "The Greatness and Decline of Rome" by Ferrero. Ferrero mentions Publius Cornelius Lentulus as a consul 58 B.C. and Lucius Cornelius Lentulus as a candidate for consulship 49 B.C.

In Ferguson's "Rome" Adam Ferguson tells of Publius Cornelius Lentulus, a praetor, in the Conspiracy of Catiline. In H. C. Havell's work entitled "Republican Rome" he describes the same Publius Cornelius Lentulus in the Conspiracy of Catiline 63 B.C.

Latimer, in a work entitled "Judea from Cyrus to Titus" 537 B.C. to 70 A.D., gives a complete chapter on Pontius Pilate, but does not mention Publius Lentulus.

Lodge, in his "History of the Nations," Volume Three, mentions Publius Lentulus and the conspiracy of 63 B.C. Cicero's Orations, by Yonge, give the same mention. The Merivale "History of the Romans," Volume Seven, contains the same mention as well as Smith in his "Dictionary of Greek and Roman Biography and Mythology." "The Story of Rome," by Mommsen, Volume Five, has a great deal to say about Lucius Lentulus who was a consul 49 B.C. when civil war was declared between Caesar and Pompey.

The "Encyclopedia Britannica" has an article on Pilate but says nothing about Publius Lentulus. It also has an article on Tiberius but makes no mention of either Lentulus. It also gives an article on the Lentulus family, but mentions none during the reign of Tiberius Caesar, 14 A.D. to 37 A.D. The "Catholic Encyclopedia" in Volume Nine, says that Publius Lentulus was supposed to have been governor of Judea before Pontius Pilate, but that there never was a governor of Jerusalem nor a procurator of Judea by the name of Lentulus. It, also, in Volume Fourteen, gives a biography of Tiberius but does not mention Publius.

Other equally reliable authorities fully establish a father and son, each named Cossus Cornelius Lentulus, during the reign of Tiberius Caesar, and very possibly one of these may have been the envoy of Caesar; or there very plausibly could have been a son, grandson, or other relative of the Publius Cornelius Lentulus of the Catiline conspiracy of 63 B.C. who was of sufficient importance to be sent on a personal mission for Tiberius Caesar, and for personal reasons of the Emperor, not entered in the records of the time. If this be true then it stands to reason that the Records of Flavius Josephus might come much closer [to] being true history than those of later writers.

Much discussion concerning this matter was aroused in the spring of 1923, in France and England by the publication of Anatole France's wonderful story "The Procurator of Judea" in his book entitled "Mother of Pearl." The Paris "Matin" published the story of the discovery of the description of Jesus Christ in which I have been interested since 1909. The "Matin" told of a description in a police report accredited to a proconsul, one Publius Lentulus, predecessor to Pilate. Anatole France describes how an exiled Roman meets Pontius Pilate and inquires if he remembers Jesus. Pilate answers that he does not. The police description quoted by France is not the same as the Lentulus description. The former states that Christ had fair hair, blue eyes, and a double pointed beard. The latter states that his eyes were gray, his hair chestnut.

In an article in the *Evening Herald* of London, in the issue of May 12, 1923, H. T. Vickers writes as follows on this subject:

"It may interest your readers to learn further details of this report. It happens that I have in my possession a bound copy of the Old and New Testaments, the Apocrypha, Book of Common Prayer, etc. which is over three hundred years old, having been variously printed between the years 1619 and 1623. It contains numerous marginal notes written in Old English and Hebrew, and among them is this very report by Publius Lentulus, giving a description of the personal characteristics, etc., of Jesus.

"The writing is in Old English, traced with a very fine pen in remarkably small characters. Unfortunately, I am unable to decipher all the words, and one or two lines have been obliterated owing to the fraying of the edge of the page on which the story appears."

Mr. Vickers goes on to say, "As a matter of further interest it may be mentioned that this entry was probably made by a clergyman, Henricus Fowler, Rector of Minchinhampton, as there is an inscription in the book to that effect, bearing the date of 1628. This gentleman has very thoughtfully added a footnote, explaining that the above description of Jesus was procured for him from the library of Sir Francis Bacon, Lord Chancellor of England, and that 'the writing and the picture of Jesus Christ was a most rare masterpiece of art.'"

With this I fully agree. Evidently the powerful magnetism of this picture was as keenly felt centuries ago as it is to-day, while its authenticity is fully established.

The one fact upon which historians agree is that descriptions of the person and the work of Jesus Christ reached the Roman senate, either by letters from Judea or by personal messenger at the instigation of Caesar. No doubt the matter I used was secured by Caesar after Pilate had become alarmed at the host following the teachings of Jesus Christ, since they multiplied to disquieting numbers, and history amply sustains the fact that Pilate himself so informed Caesar, very probably because of the agitation among the High Priests over the miracles performed by Jesus, and because Herod was uneasy.

After such a letter from the governor of Judea to the Emperor of Rome, it is the most natural thing conceivable that Caesar should send a personal envoy to make an investigation, because if the power of Pilate, holding office under Herod and paying tribute to Rome, were threatened, very possibly the throne of Caesar might be threatened also. I am sure, from a study of the history of the reign of Tiberius Caesar, that he kept himself personally informed and that he made no move to prevent the death of Christ because His power with the people was a menace to Pilate and Herod, as well as to himself. The world is full of similar history. Our day need not stand aghast at the deeds of either Herod or Caesar. They have had many predecessors and successors who only needed a Christ to execute; failing this, they attempted to stabilize their official positions and extend their power by executing other rulers and their fellow men.

The Methodist Book Concern, which reproduced the "Lentulus Legend," had taken the liberty slightly to alter the matter, and in my use of it in the early part of the poem, in order to swing it to the rhythm and meter selected, still further liberties were taken with the structure, but only minor ones, and in no instance was the sense even slightly altered.

Gibbon, in "The Decline and Fall of the Roman Empire," Volume Two, Chapter Sixteen, Page 108, according to the fifth edition issued by Methuen and Company of London, has this to say: "The apology of Tertullian contains two very ancient, very singular, but at the same time, very suspicious, instances of Imperial clemency; the edicts published by Tiberius and Marcus Antoninus, and designed not only to protect the innocence of the Christians, but even to proclaim those stupendous miracles which had attested the truth of their doctrine. The first of these examples is attended with some difficulties which might perplex the skeptical mind. We are required to believe that Pontius Pilate informed the emperor of the unjust sentence of death which he had pronounced against an innocent, and, as it appeared, a divine person; and that, without acquiring the merit, he exposed himself to the danger of martyrdom; that Tiberius, who avowed his contempt for all religion, immediately conceived the design of placing the Jewish Messiah among the gods of Rome; that his servile senate ventured to disobey the commands of their master; that Tiberius, instead of resenting their refusal, contented himself with protecting the Christians from the severity of the laws, many years before such laws were enacted, or before the church had assumed any distinct name or existence; and lastly, that the memory of this extraordinary transaction was preserved in the most public and authentic records, which escaped the knowledge of the historians of Greece and Rome, and were only visible to the eyes of an African Christian, who composed his apology one hundred and sixty years after the death of Tiberius." If this astounding fact escaped the knowledge of the historians of Greece and Rome, other facts equally important might very much well have escaped or been concealed from them also. One thing is certain: there is some basic truth—at the beginning of every Legend. Gibbon continues: "The edict of Marcus Antoninus is supposed to have been the effect of his devotion and gratitude for the miraculous deliverance which he had obtained in the Marcomannic war."

This sustains my conception of Tiberius Caesar in the foregoing poem. Given proof that Pilate informed Tiberius Caesar of the appearance and work of Jesus Christ, it is altogether probable that Caesar should have looked to his own security by sending a personal envoy minutely to investigate the person and the teachings of the man who threatened the rule of Pilate and incurred the wrath of Herod and the High Priests led by Cephas. That Pilate sent several letters to Caesar and to the Roman senate is unquestionable. The several Biblical records of the crucifixion all make clear the fact that Pilate tried in various ways to influence the High Priests and the Elders to save Jesus. The wife of Pilate entered a plea for the life of Jesus. Pilate himself used all his influence to secure the release of Jesus instead of Barabbas, and when all appeals failed, publicly performed the ceremony of washing his hands of the whole affair. That Caesar had been deeply moved by the report brought to him concerning the person and the work of Jesus Christ and by the subsequent nobility and attitude of His followers, is amply proved by Caesar's many acts of clemency to the Christians even in defiance of the rulings of the senate. In this I find ample and substantial ground for my conception as to how the likeness of Jesus of the Emerald was produced.

"Birds of the Bible" was published in 1909. In March of 1922 I received a packet from Mr. Charles Anderson, of Melbourne, Australia, containing what was to me a new likeness of Jesus Christ. The sender stated that thirty years ago, while in the employ of the British Museum, he had secured the privilege of making a copy of a negative which had been photographed from a priceless emerald now held among the treasures of the Vatican. He wrote that he had been reading "Birds of the Bible" and the Lentulus legend he found there so perfectly fitted the picture in his possession that he felt I would be interested. This photograph made one of two things evident. Either the description was written from it, or it had been drawn to fit the description. In either case there was no questioning the fact that the description and the picture belonged together. I was delighted with the picture because it fulfilled my personal conception of Jesus Christ developed from early teaching and subsequent investigation.

Those who believe the Biblical account of the birth of Jesus Christ must concede that the plan of God for the salvation of this world was to have a Son of His own conceived by an immaculate virgin and brought into this world in the same manner as all little children, that he might reach maturity understanding the nature and having had the experience of other men of the world; that He should fulfil the mission for which He was sent and return to his Father. As the Son of God there was no reason why Jesus Christ should have resembled other men of His time and His mother's race. It is specifically stated that He was the Son of God, sent to save all men — Greek, Hebrew, Roman. It is urgently reasonable that in such case his power would be greater with all men if, in appearance, he possessed the perfection of a God, rather than to resemble closely any particular race, many of these races having been for ages at war.

There is every reason why He should have resembled God, His Father. An inscription photographed with the likeness states: "The only true likeness of 'Our Saviour' taken from one cut on an emerald by command of Tiberius Caesar, and given from the Treasury of Constantinople by the Emperor of the Turks to Pope Innocent VIII for the redemption of his brother, then a captive of the Christians."

This does not explain why so beautiful and appealing a picture should not long ago have been given general circulation. The real reason probably lies in the fact that some historians do not believe in the authenticity of the likeness. Since every other picture we possess of Jesus Christ is merely the idea of some artist as to how the Saviour looked when He performed His mission in human form among us, I can see no reason why the conception of Him by the particular artist who made this picture should be suppressed and others, emanating from no more reliable sources, should be exploited. To my mind there is the strongest possibility that both the description and the picture are genuine, that the description might have been attributed to a Lentulus one generation later, the first Publius being definitely located 63 B.C.

I have shown this likeness to no one of any race or denomination who ever before had seen or heard of it with the exception of Bishop Cantwell of the Diocese of Los Angeles. The Bishop told me that many years ago, while travelling in Australia, he had seen a copy of this picture in the possession of a man of that country. He also knew of the original emerald among the treasures of the Vatican. Mrs. [Carrie] Nation, who spent twenty years of her life in Rome gathering the collection of reproductions of the great sacred paintings of the world recently purchased by the City of New York, told me personally that she had seen the emerald, engraved with the head of Christ, among the treasures of the Vatican, and had been permitted to handle it. Recently, Tiffany's, in collecting treasures for the Morgan Memorial Hall of the American Museum of Natural History of New York, purchased from the estate of a woman to whom a cardinal had given it, a head of Jesus cut on an orange garnet one and a quarter by one and three quarter inches in dimension. This head is entirely lacking in the spiritual appeal, the exquisite curves of line and feature which mark the likeness of Jesus of the Emerald. I have discussed this subject with many prelates of standing and none of them can see any conceivable reason why this wonderful likeness of Jesus should not be given to His followers as well as other attempts by other artists to materialize Him physically.

It is a matter of speculation among students as to how the minute work of the ancients in carving so exquisitely the extremely hard stones, spoken of by them as "living stones," was accomplished without the aid of lenses. Such work was for a time a lost art which revived with the manufacture of lenses. The "living stones" of the ancients were those least affected by fire or water—the diamond, the sapphire, topaz, ruby, emerald, and so forth. In another class they listed the pearl, sardonyx, turquoise, and stones of softer formation.

I never have shown this likeness of Jesus Christ to any one of any denomination, or of none at all, who did not instantly pause and study it in tense absorption, nor have I yet found any one capable of putting into words exactly the appeal made to him by this face. The phrase of the Lentulus description concerning the nose and mouth "so marked as cannot be described" might well apply to the entire face, so exquisite is the appeal of its God-like beauty, its purity and compassion.

I can see no reason, since it never fails to make this appeal, why it should not be placed in the hands of every believer in the immaculate conception; of every lover of the personality and the teachings of Jesus Christ. It will be recalled that in our translations of the history of the mission of Christ on this earth there is a hiatus. No one gives any explanation of where Jesus was or how He occupied His time after He taught the doctors of the law in the temple until He made His appearance at the beginning of His ministry. A clue has been offered by Nicholas Notovitch which can be found in a French translation by Alexina Loranger in a little booklet entitled "The Unknown Life of Jesus Christ." This link was supplied by Notovitch who, while travelling in the East, found among the records of a monastery in Thibet at Himis a memoir of the life of Jesus Christ which indicates that the period concerning which our records give no history was spent in a long journey on the part of Jesus, during which He sailed on trading vessels to far countries and there talked with the people, preaching the same doctrines, the same plan of salvation, as He later preached in Judea. These records state that Jesus secretly left His father's house, went out of Jerusalem in the company of some merchants and travelled to Sind that He might study the religion, the laws, and the customs of other countries. He was taught the languages and beliefs of many peoples. He later spent six years in Benaires and other holy cities continuing His journey through India, and the records found there concerning Him exactly coincide with the teachings that He later spread throughout Judea and they also explain His breadth of vision, His depth of understanding, His authoritative speech, and a broader comprehension than He could have attained had He remained during these nineteen years in His humble home in Bethlehem, working at the trade of a carpenter, except by direct miracle such as He displayed in the temple of Jerusalem at the age of twelve. These translations show that He taught in these foreign countries that He was the Son of God, that in the course of time He must return to His own land, and if need be, offer Himself as a sacrifice for the redemption of His people; and the records also show that news of His crucifixion was carried back to these foreign countries and that they deeply mourned the death of one whose teachings they respected and whom they considered a saint. It appeals to me that savants interested in ancient research could find no more promising matter than by going through the archives of these ancient monasteries of India, Thibet, and the lands visited by Jesus, and searching for other chronicles such as that brought from Thibet by Nicholas Notovitch.

Before writing "Folk Lore of the Bible" Frasier made the most extensive travel and research of any man aspiring to authority on this subject. He not only circled the globe, but he spent the greater part of an average lifetime visiting the most remote peoples, and everywhere he found in the hearts of men a universal belief in a great ruling Spirit. He found very similar beliefs and customs practised all over the world, based on very similar lines of reasoning. He also found widespread a knowledge of the sunken Atlantis and traditions of the flood even among widely scattered tribes of our North American Indians. He found far-reaching knowledge of the world's two greatest records of abatement of natural law in the star that travelled eastward and stood still over Bethlehem at the birth of Christ, and the even greater phenomenon of the hours in which the world was enveloped in darkness at the time of the crucifixion.

To my mind it is absurd to look to the Heavens above us and believe that other innumerable bodies circling their orbits, other suns, other moons, other solar systems, can differ widely from ours. The spectrum now shows thirty suns surrounded by planetary systems. In the nature of things they must be formed practically of the same substances as is our world; they must evolve life in the same way. I do not understand how there can be any doubt in the mind of any one touching natural science even lightly that these other worlds, many of them larger and more favourably situate in the universe than we, have evolved life and living conditions and have been peopled possibly aeons before our time. The spectrum now points to Venus as showing the most signs of having living conditions of any planet near us.

Neither in my mind is there any doubt but that God, at the right time and in His own way, has worked out for these other worlds the same plan of salvation that has been vouchsafed to us. In the economy of Nature nothing is ever lost. I cannot believe that the soul of man shall prove the one exception. I do believe in Jesus Christ, in His mission among us, in the breadth of that mission, and I do believe this picture of Jesus of the Emerald to be the closest reproduction, up to this time, of the face of the man who lived the life and performed the works that history proves were achieved by Jesus Christ.

Moved to the depths of my soul by the spiritual appeal of this beautiful attempt to materialize Jesus Christ as a physical man, the foregoing conception of how it might have been produced was born in my heart and brain, and because of the compelling power of the picture I am moved to share it with all the world who believe in Jesus Christ.

"Euphorbia"

"Euphorbia" appeared serially in *Good Housekeeping*: Part I, 76 (January 1923): 10–13, 115–21; Part II, 76 (Feb. 1923): 24–27, 121–22, 125–26, 128–31; Part III, 76 (March 1923): 42–45, 122, 125–26,128. According to Porter's daughter, Jeanette Meehan, it "was the first poem ever published serially in a magazine and, . . . Mother was paid for it more than was ever paid for any poem published" (Meehan, 246). In this hymn to the landscape of California, Porter has told a story of hardship and abuse, finally abated and healed by sunshine, wildflowers, and compassion. Still experimenting with poetics, she wrote in a letter to Mrs. Pennebaker, "Through the first instalment of the poem, and probably half of the next instalment, the rhythms are broken. It was a struggle. Everywhere 'Marge' turned she was defeated. She was like a bird battering her wings against the cage of Life." Then, as the story resolves, the meter becomes more regular (Meehan, 251).

PART I

It was a long, rough road from Kennebunk,
Lying near the rocky coast of harsh Maine
To the Sunland desert of California,
As Jacob L. and Margery Travers
Made the halting, pain-punctured journey.
Their pilgrimage was scarcely straighter

Than the course of the children of Israel.
But it required only twenty-seven years
For Jacob and Margery to reach Sunland.

When they started, Jacob was twenty-two,
A well-built man firm-standing on straight legs,
Having broad shoulders and capable hands,
His head finely shaped, his face expressive.
His deep-set, gray eyes looked upon the world
With deliberation presaging shrewdness.

Margery was a sweet bride at seventeen;
Her luring features were rough, wavy hair
And big, dark-brown eyes, mellow and patient.

They were deeply in love with each other
When they left the rocks and fish of Kennebunk
For the promising vineyards of New York.
Two years of growing grapes wearied Jacob,
So he tried oil in Pennsylvania.
The long road was mountainous and wearing,
While as an oil magnate, he failed sooner
Than in the vineyards of dissatisfaction.

Then he tested the farm lands of Ohio,
But his beginning was unfortunate
Because the locusts descended in swarms
And sheared the grain and vegetables to earth.
The curse of Jacob fell on Ohio;
He hated it with such burning hatred
That in putting satisfying distance
Between himself and its blighting locusts
He hurried past intervening richness
And paused with homing intent in Kansas.

The first year presaged great prosperity;
The second, grasshoppers ravaged like locusts;
The third, the tremendous wrath of a cyclone

So nearly blew them from the hated state
That they continued the enforced journey
To the cotton lands of Arizona.

By the time they encountered the hot suns
And the alkali waters awaiting them,
Jacob was a grizzled, surly misanthrope,
Ready to blame his hard luck on his country,
On God, on the weather, on Margery,
Who was not responsible for any of it.
She had endured her thwarted existence,
Moving when Jacob decreed that they should.

When at last they settled in Arizona
They were storm-weathered, middle-aged people.
Jacob resembled an impregnable rock
That unceasing rip-tides had tormented
And the sun had scorched past the endurance
Of any mitigating veiling of lichen;
But he gave the determined impression
Of a man who did some essential work.

Margery had sown her beauty broadcast:
The luster had left her hair in Ohio,
The red had failed lip and cheek in Kansas,
And the roundness had worn from her figure
In valiant battles with prairie muck,
On unnumbered miles of rocky highways,
With the fierce sands of relentless deserts.
Even her lilting name shrank to harsh "Marge."

Nine small graves dotted beside the highway
Marked the bitterness of her pilgrimage,
While its end found her weary arms empty.

She never had kept even one baby
Long enough to grow so familiar with it
That she could select a suitable name.

To Marge the tiny creatures were numerals—
Number one, pain and sorrow in New York,
Two and three, the same in Pennsylvania,
Up to number nine in Arizona,
Accounting for almost anything in Marge.

She had forgotten, in these weary years,
That the world had held such a thing as love;
Life had left her only stolid endurance.
It never occurred to Marge's mentality
That after she had ceased to love Jacob
There was no reason for remaining with him,
Dragging from one hopeless venture to another,
Following the dictates of his fancy.

Marge was so sick of Arizona that,
For the first time since leaving Kennebunk,
She began another advance on sunset
With a sigh closely resembling relief.
She felt that it would be unreasonable
For country that lay nearer the ocean
To be so difficult to exist in;
And if it were even slightly better
There was at least the possibility
That life with Jacob might be easier.

Jacob experienced in his selfish heart
The keenest exultation he had known,
Because his small share of Arizona
Had lain within the radius of the land
Desired by a great eastern syndicate
For an experiment in cotton growing.
The price he got for his sun-bitten acres
Made him the most cash in hand at one time
He ever had possessed during his life.

He became so deeply dissatisfied
With all the former ventures he had made

That his thoughts turned hungrily back to Maine;
He could not understand why he had left.
He realized that the far road to youth
Was too long and too rough to retravel,
But he longed past his powers of denial
For the healing consolation of the sea;
So on the morning of their final move
He grimly turned his hunched back to the sun
And drove his discouraged team straight westward.

Marge knew no more of his destination
Than the worn blankets or the cooking pots.
She was not given the pleasure of feeling
That she was destined for California;
Nor was she told what sum was in the belt
That at night she felt girding Jacob's loins.

Day after day she lay on the comforts,
Grinding through the dusty, evasive sand.
Pounding over the resisting mountain roads,
Until she lost desire to know the time:
Each day was so similar to the past,
All of them so devoid of cause for hope.

After enduring uncounted weeks of this,
There came at last a memorable morning,
When the tired horses were unable to climb farther,
On which the weary road changed suddenly.
It began to wind down colorful mountains;
It slowly crossed cool, alluring valleys
And crept through crisp flower-bedecked canyons,
Companioned by gaily-singing cold water.

Then signs of civilization blended:
Cultivated patches like gay carpets
In delicate, green-veiled pastel colors,
Spread on the sides of the maroon mountains;
Little fields of anemic, discouraged corn,

Squat adobe lodges of terra cotta,
The flat roofs gold with drying husked corn,
The walls festooned with strings of red peppers.
Indians, wearing the trousers of today
And the flaming head-band of the wild,
Passed them on the way to the rocky fields,
Or, with well-filled quiver and shining bow,
Going to the chase as their grandfathers,
Because of the price of ammunition.

Farther on they came to Mexican homes,
To short, brown people living hardily;
And then to lean, struggling, white families.
One day Marge got the small satisfaction
Of learning that Jacob was going west
Until he came to the Pacific Ocean.

Marge experienced her first thrill in years.
She had known the Atlantic in her youth;
The Pacific would be quite similar.
It would be clean; it would have movement.
There would be growing things lining its shores,
And great, wide-winged birds of white and gray
Circling and soaring high among the clouds.
After that, Marge rode with her feet dangling
From the back end of the lurching wagon,
Keenly appraising the homes that they passed.

A few of these reviving, healing new days
Brought them to miles of nut and fruit orchards;
The breeze suggested lemon and pepper.
With head alert and distended nostrils
Marge sniffed the familiar, cooling salt air.

One day she felt the mist-breath of the sea.
In a world of flowers, of endless green,
She cried out, "Oh Jacob, I smell the sea."
Jacob made scornful and surly reply,

"You have been smelling it all morning long,
But you were too pudden-headed to know it!"

Then Marge slid over the end gate at once
And walked many inspiring miles eagerly
On resilient black roads smooth as barn floors,
Because her body demanded exercise.
In spite of more than three thousand tired miles
Of vastly unpropitious journeyings
A germ of hope was working in her breast.

Jacob kept his word, as he always did
When his pledges were made to himself.
He drove steadily ahead until the surf
Broke foaming at the dragging feet of his horses.
He camped and rested for a few short days,
Then he began studying the prices of land.

Had Jacob been any one except himself
His eyes would have thoroughly informed him,
Long before the benediction of the sea,
That he was passing all available land;
But Jacob was a peculiar man,
Who only learned that he was on rough footing
When he suddenly fell flat and very hard.

The first half-day with realty agents
Left him sore and in bitterness of spirit,
Beginning to curse California.
The end of the day found him in fighting mood,
Because every penny in his loin belt
Could not purchase one acre of the land
Close to the pictures and music of the sea.

There was nothing remaining for Jacob
But to face the patient horses toward sun-up
And travel back until he reached the place
Where he could buy land upon which to live.

Another day taught him convincingly
That the soil he purchased must be virgin,
Since the price of cleared land was prohibitive;
So Jacob and Marge faced east with sick hearts
And drearily retraced their alluring route
Until they reached the vicinity of Sunland.

The curses Jacob had spent on Ohio
Multiplied like a ball of tumble-weed
When he began passing the rocky vineyards
And the stone-covered, scorched clearings
In which men pitted themselves against Nature.
Jacob threw up his hands and cried to Heaven:
"Stone foundations, stone houses, stone walls,
Stones in ricks and heaps, stones and yet more stones!
Great God, why did You put all the damned things
In Maine, New York, and California:
Have I dragged us from ocean to ocean
Only to reach a land of grapes and stones?"
Yet cultivated Sunland was attractive,
Big eucalyptus and pepper trees remained.
The unfolding ocean air was reviving;
The stories men told of what could be done
With desert land began to appease Jacob.
Marge rode blindly, hating each hope-quenching mile.

Near the far eastern outskirts of Sunland,
Where primal desert lay as it had lain
Since only the God of Nature knows when,
Jacob found a spot that his money could purchase
And leave enough to build a small house
In which to live while they cleared the land.

To Marge the situation seemed hopeless
When she faced Jacob's latest investment;
When she looked at the land adjoining,
Two years under careful cultivation,
Hope would stir faintly in her heart again.

All they needed was sufficient water,
In order to grow anything they wanted
In the rocky, sandy soil of Sunland;
And proved the statements past cavil
By pointing out where blessed water flowed,
And allowing orchards, vineyards, gardens,
To speak in oranges, grapes, and potatoes.

Jacob paid cash for five acres of desert
Lying beside the level Sunland highway—
Desert in front, to the horizon,
Desert to the right in a small section;
To the left, three cleared and cultivated acres
Belonging to their nearest neighbor.

When Jacob stopped in the southwest corner,
Announcing that he would build their home there,
Marge climbed from the wagon to hunt firewood;
The air had made her wolfishly hungry.
She ventured the suggestion to Jacob
That a better location for their home
Would be nearer to the middle of the land
So that the water required for living
Could irrigate larger space around them,
And they could keep closer guard on their crops.

Jacob's opinion of a woman's mind
Was so negative in its nature
That he did not even listen to Marge.
He went where a contractor was working
And arranged for him to erect a small house.

As far as Marge could gather from their plans,
Water from far-reaching Los Angeles mains
Would be her only real convenience.
While the house was being hastily built
She slept in the wagon, cooked near it,

And worked shoulder-even with Jacob,
Clearing for the planting of their garden.

How Marge kept her little germ of hope alive
Would be an extremely difficult thing
For the uninitiated to fathom.
The sun falls penetrantly on Sunland;
There is evident reason for its name.
The roots of desert growth strike straight and deep,
Reaching, always reaching downward, for moisture.
Here, the fight for life is so desperate
That when drouth and heat have been overcome
The desert intends to run no further risk;
By the million it throws out protective spurs,
Its lances, its bayonets, its spears, its spines,
And its needles, steel strong, fine and sharp.

When Jacob went to buy boots for himself
To protect his feet and legs from punishment,
He did see the just necessity
Of getting a durable pair for Marge.
That they were too large and blistered her feet,
That they were heavy and needlessly tired her,
Were matters far outside Jacob's province.
He had not felt so virtuous in years
As when he presented the boots to Marge.
Marge put them on, pinned up her scant skirts,
Took her mattock in hand, and gravely went forth
To challenge the desert to deadly warfare.

In only a few days their house was finished—
A slight frame, weatherboarded outside,
Sealed with pine stripping on the inside,
A shingled roof, three small, hopeless rooms,
And it was completed, having two virtues:
It was shelter, and it was clean and new.
The one luxury was the hydrant
Which would water them and the garden.

When Jacob went to town for furnishings,
Marge willingly remained to grub greasewood.
She had no desire to go where she would see
Miracles of conveniences not for her;
Better to stay at home and do what she could
With Jacob's purchases when he brought them.

But, on his speedy return, she was aghast
At the trash he piled on the veranda.
She was not given time for cleaning;
The dreadful bedstead and the rusty stove,
The uncertain table and the wobbly chairs
Were put into place wearing the grime of years.

Jacob brought in and set on their western line
A hedge of eucalyptus for firewood.
There was gas, but he had the wood habit
And no sympathy for the trials of the cook.
He adorned the front yard with one pepper tree
Without making any comment to Marge.
It was quite unnecessary that he should:
The pepper tree disdained all apology.

One more concession Jacob made to his soul.
Somewhere deep in his inner consciousness
He dreamed a dream of an ideal home.
The house he visioned was white and roomy;
There were lights in the windows at night;
An inviting walk led to the front door;
There were a grassy lawn, a neat picket fence,
And firmly fixed in Jacob's dream home
There were substantial but ornate gate-posts.
Between them swung a wide, welcoming gate,
The daily passing through the portals of which,
To a Jacob of a different caliber
Having a soul of workable fabric,
Would have been a sacred ceremonial.

Jacob's soul was so warped by circumstance
And through following his natural desires
That, although it demanded the gate,
Very likely, to have saved his soul,
He could not have explained the real reason;
But the urge for the gate was in his brain
Until he was driven to fare forth,
After a day of hard wrestling with clearing,
To search the desert for timber for gate-posts.

The quest seemed so absurd at the start
That each day he grew more discouraged.
Finally he compromised on large branches
Secured from a trimmed pepper tree down the road.
The gate he constructed from odd pieces
Remaining after the building was finished.
The thickness varied, also the length and width,
But every one passing on the highway
Felt that the result of Jacob's work
Was intended for gate-posts and a gate.

Travelers knew also that the building
At the end of the planks that led to it
Was meant to be a house, was built for a home;
It matched the gate-posts beautifully.
Halfway down the walk from the front door
Spread a queer, little mat of reddish green,
The only living thing left in the cleared space
That had escaped Jacob's grubbing mania—
A small weed saved by its obscurity.

Back of the house there was a shack for the horses,
Glad beasts, having a real rest while they waited
Their time to set their breasts against the desert.
When the sweet, cold water of the mountains
Began to flow over their land lavishly,
And the garden space was cleared and seeded,
The larger task of the remainder faced them.

Jacob plunged into this strenuous work
As if he had encountered a fierce enemy.
He ripped and tore, he delved and cursed profusely;
But he reached the thread roots of every greasewood,
Each sage brush and mesquite in his way.
Yucca and madrona made no appeal to him;
They were merely pests delaying rich crops
That he might grow and turn into money
At the small wholesale station half a mile below.
Cacti he hated with fierce, snarling hatred.
He cursed the cholla, root, stem, and needles;
He banged the bisnaga with a shovel.
He coined new oaths never heard on the desert
To expend on the great growths of nopal
Holding over his head menacing needles
Which had back at him with enthusiasm.
Jacob, working his way across his five acres,
Resembled an enraged sabre-toothed tiger
Such as had fought over the same location
Only a very few ages earlier.

Marge began at the edge of the garden
And made her eastward way in a wide swathe.
She tackled the alder and the scrub oak
As enthusiastically as Jacob;
She hated the cacti armor as deeply;
But she could not strike down the great growths
Without pausing over the exquisite gold,
The dull red, the delicate pink of their bloom.

Marge had no time for self-analysis;
She did not know that life had failed for her
Because it lacked color and cadence.
Now the desert supplied the color. . . .
She saw it in little hills of green
From silvery sage to darkest olive,
Touched with the varying purple of lupin,
The vivid red of penstemon and larkspur,
Splashed with small seas of ever-shifting gold,

All blended with the pastel of cacti.
Marge saw dazing sunrise and sunset colors
On endless ranges of changing mountains,
Floating cloud banners of soft, smoky gray
From crests of blue or rose or lavender.

Her ear was wholly untrained in wild notes,
But slowly it began picking up cadence.
Something in the desert was hourly singing,
A slow, soft song of tender heart-ease;
Something answered on the mountains,
A clear, hearty note of reassurance.
The winds voiced every mood of Nature
As they sang over her quiescent desert.
Some days Marge heard low, soothing sea notes;
Some days they rose to forceful insistence;
Again they trumpeted with thunder tones.
The combination began to comfort her
For the silent surliness of Jacob.

Each hour her eye grew alert in responding
To color she never before had seen.
Her heart pulsed faster in welling throbs
To music, mostly the voice of Nature
But in small part a little personal song
Of the slowly awakening soul of her.
She knew that cacti and lupin interfered
With cultivated gardens and orchards,
But she had seen so little of beauty
That her hand rebelled before she struck.

She never had paused in one homing place
Long enough to watch the growth of a tree.
No shrub had reached maturity for her.
Sometimes she had grown annual flowers,
But they had been hardy and commonplace.
Petunias, nasturtiums, portulacca,
Had encompassed her previous efforts.

Working her way down the line of the desert,
She often paused to study living colors.
Reluctantly she uprooted any flowers;
When she reached her first blooming penstemon,
"The humming-birds' dinner-horn" of botanists—
That one having exquisite, silver-red stems
And lance-shaped, frosty, blue-green leaves of wonder
Similar to young oat fields of Ohio,
With hundreds of little, red, fluted horns
Delicately hung on the vivid sprays,
Before which the humming-birds poised on air—
She paused in a ferment of inward revolt.

At that instant Jacob came prowling her way.
"Are you staring at a gila monster?" he cried.
Marge drew a deep, uncertain breath of protest
That slightly lifted her lean shoulders.
"I was only thinking," she said quietly.

Jacob glanced at her speculatively;
He knew very well what she was thinking.
It was her duty to have been thinking,
Had she been like women he approved,
How large a space she could clear in a day,
How thoroughly she could grub out deep roots,
How many fruits and vegetables she could grow;
And it was evident that she was not.
She was thinking that the thing before her
Was something of such alluring beauty
That she hated to strike out its life.

In pursuance of his daily custom
During the period of their years together,
Jacob instantly made up Marge's mind for her.
He obligingly struck in her stead;
With a sweep of the shovel he was carrying
He sheared the humming-birds' dinner horn
Level with the sands of the desert.

A hard look crept over Marge's sunburned face;
A half-sob rose in her pulsing throat;
Angry words flocked to her close-shut lips.
Silently she bent, struck the mattock deep,
And worked out the roots of the penstemon.

Jacob went his way quite pleased with himself.
"How like Marge—mooning over a flower
When she should have been preparing a patch
For cabbage and potatoes!" he muttered.

Marge drove her mattock deep into the earth;
She circled the penstemon widely.
Then she dropped on her knees, bent forward,
And began carefully easing up the roots.
A half-smile twisted her firmly-set lips
At the thought of what Jacob would say.
"Just as well to cut the tops," she argued;
Comforting her heart against desecration.
"Couldn't have moved it in full bloom anyway.
This will make it easier for both of us."
Then Marge hid the roots under an alder
Out of range of the line she was working.

After that she cleared in absorbed interest,
For Life had mercifully intervened,
Setting upon her the seal of Beauty.
In those days her eyes ranged far ahead of her,
Always engaged in eager, concealed search.
When she sighted the slender, blood-red
Of a tall, glowing mast of larkspur,
The tissue white of that thistle poppy
So cleverly designated as "fried eggs,"
Or the delicate pink lace of filaree,
Or a dwarfed bunch of amber tidy-tips,
She watched Jacob, and when he was not looking,
She topped the flowers and added the roots
To the heap in the shade of the alder.

When she found her first bush of roméro,
Marge involuntarily cried aloud.
Jacob raised his head and shouted angrily,
"Can't you work without murdering yourself?"

Marge looked at the plant and smiled to it,
The kind of smile one gives a little child
When one is coaxing for a lovely response.
Her eyes wandered from the unique flowers
To the clusters of narrow leaves, also strange.
The rich green of the thick outer margins
Curled over the white wool of the lining,
The sprays of gay flowers branching widely,
Exquisite, fluted, blue tubes an inch in length,
The stamens, half a dozen in number,
Coiling away beyond the corolla,
Full bloom, half bloom, quarter bloom, then slanting
Up to huddled buds of pinkish purple,
The whole spray veiled with clotted violet wool,
Forming a mist of the loveliest color
Marge ever had seen on any growing thing.

She dug close to the roméro with breathless care,
Leaving it till Jacob shouldered his tools
And started to the house at supper time.
Then she cut the long, pinkish-blue flower sprays
And raised the roots with exquisite precision.
She had a heavy load in her dress skirt
When she hurried homeward behind Jacob.
She hid the roots in a dark, sheltered place
And cooked supper as quickly as she could.

After Jacob had gulped his food greedily,
He immediately strolled down the street
In search of companionship of his kind,
To the fruit stall and corner grocery.
Marge speedily washed the heavy dishes,

And, drawing a straight line from the gateposts
To each end of the space allowed for a yard,
She began setting the roots on either side.

She would complete Jacob's decoration
By growing a hedge of flowering wildlings.
On one side she would put the roméro
And everything of related color;
On the other she would use the penstemon,
The red larkspur, and all the bloody blooms;
Down the sunny side of the house, in a bed,
She would plant the other insistent flowers.

She did not know what her specimens were;
With the perception born in a botanist
She called the penstemon "humming-birds' flower"
Because those birds were numerous around it;
And the roméro, with long, curved, blue stamens,
She named "blue-curls" the same as would you or I.

She was desperately tired when she finished.
She looked at the long line of her planting,
And then, with a whimsical smile on her lips,
Instead of stepping over the rescued roots,
She walked down the line, passing through the gate,
Following Jacob's invariable custom;
Suddenly the gate was justified to her.

As she came down the walk, facing the house,
Half-way to the porch that sheltered the front door,
Marge for the first time really noticed
The appealing, little, spreading, red plant.
Her shovel was set, ready to uproot it;
Then she hesitated and looked closely.
She had been hurt so much in her own life
That it tortured all her finer instincts
To strike down a thing of living beauty.

The color-splashed mat, strangely appealing,
Sprawling in contentment beside the walk,
Caught and held her definite attention.
She stood studying it, and then slowly,
And tired though she was, she knelt beside it.
Her hands hovered over it in a caress;
A warm smile softened her severe, lined face.
"Why, you pretty little thing, you!" she said slowly.

She seated herself on the walk,
Studying the wine-colored stems of the plant,
The tiny, maroon flowers edged with rosy white,
The delicate, heart-shaped, curving, little leaves
Set so precisely in opposition,
With their shading of rare green, brown mottled,
Neatly bound by a narrow line of white.

She carefully slipped her cracked, gnarled fingers
Under a fine spray for close inspection.
"I don't see how Jacob could lay this walk
Without tramping the life out of you," said Marge.
She sat a long time visiting the flower—
Sat until the mocking birds began to sing,
Until the rosy finches went to sleep,
And the moon peeped at her over the mountains—
Sat until the chilled night made her bones ache.

Then she arose and went into the house;
At the back door she washed and took a drink.
She was moving in deep preoccupation,
But she revealed the real trend of her thought
When, before undressing to go to bed,
She dragged her feet half the length of the walk
And poured a quart of water on the plant.

The next time the neighbor adjoining them
Stopped in passing to proffer friendship,

Marge pointed out the variegated mat.
"Do you know what that little thing is?" she asked.

Lucy Martin glanced at it casually.
"Why sure," she said; "every one here knows about that.
You're in luck to have a good thrifty one
Growing so conveniently at your door.
That's a cure of ancient Greece for many poisons.
The Indians around here have always used it
For rattlers, side-winders, and tarantulas."
"For land's sake!" cried Marge, deeply amazed,
Her eyes brilliant with intense interest.
"You know, I nearly used the shovel on it;
Then I saw how mighty attractive it was,
How pretty and dainty, and so many colors,
So different from everything else,
That I carried water to it instead.
Do you happen to know the name of it?"

"Yes, for a wonder," said Lucy, "I do.
It has the very prettiest name of all.
I don't know why I always remember it
Unless it is on account of the snakes:
They kind of made an impression on me.
I don't know many of these desert flowers
Except lupin and cactus and thistle-sage;
But the name of this is euphorbia."

"'Eu-phor-bi-a'" repeated Marge slowly,
Forming the syllables with exacting lips.
"That is an awful pretty name," she said;
"And some way it seems to suit the flower.
Do you know a bird over in the desert
Speaks that word as plainly as I can say it?
'Eu-phor-bi-a,' it keeps calling all day.
Maybe it wanted me to know about it.
How do the Indians use it for snake bites?"

"Easiest way imaginable," said Lucy.
"Pound the euphorbia until the milk runs;
Take a knife and cut deep each side the bite;
Slap the sticky, white mess on, bind it fast,
Forget it and go about your business."
"Sounds simple enough," commented Marge,
Staring at the little plant inquiringly.
"I wonder if it truly would do any good."

"Sure it would," said Lucy Martin earnestly.
"The Indians use it for more than snake poison;
They know how it works from experience:
Most medicine we use we got from them."

Marge studied the euphorbia; then she said:
"They told us about rattlers and side-winders
Coiled under the shade of shrubs and dead wood.
If snakes should strike or tarantulas bite,
It would be our first piece of perfect luck
To have the plant that would save our lives
Growing so conveniently before our door."

Part II

After that, Marge visited the euphorbia
Every time she passed its location.
The grateful plant speedily gave proof that
While it could exist with little water
It appreciated having an abundance.
It began to brighten, to run over the sand.
Its flowers and leaves doubled in size;
Their white margining was more strikingly defined;
Its stems showed a more vivid maroon.

And then, just when she had come to regard it
With more real affection than she felt
For any other living thing on earth,
Jacob one day appeared unexpectedly
And caught her pouring water on it.

"Why the hell are you wasting water
We need for the garden on weeds?" he shouted.
For the first time in recent memory
Marge smiled at Jacob dissemblingly;
She tried in a stumbling way to placate him.

"I forgot to show this to you," she said.
"It's our biggest piece of luck in years.
You know they told us how like it was
That a rattler might get us in the clearing;
And Lucy Martin says this is a sure cure.
If you get a bite, you just make a clean cut
On each side of it, deep as the fangs sink;
Then you pound a piece of this to sticky paste,
Bind it on, and then forget all about it.
Lucy said so. She said it was a sure cure."

Jacob growled: "I ain't going to have that weed
Right here in the front yard. No, ma'am!"
"Well, so long as there is nothing else," said Marge,
"I shouldn't think you would mind it so much."

Jacob advanced on the euphorbia,
Malicious intent plain on face and figure.
Marge bravely held out a restraining hand:
"You'd better not," she warned earnestly,
"Might get a bite *yourself.* This is awful rare.
You haven't seen any like it; now, have you?
I've seen only this one, with careful watching,
And it's a sure cure for tarantulas, too!
It would be foolish as throwing down your gun
When a bear was coming, to pull it up."

Jacob stopped for sufficient reason:
What Marge said was extremely feasible.
It was plain sense of the common horse kind.
He drew a step closer and studied the plant:
In his mind he was saying to himself
That he would know euphorbia after that,

And if he found it growing any place else,
He would remember the spot for safety
And then pull up Marge's merely to spite her.

Just when, in his career as Marge's husband,
Jacob reached the point where he ceased to love her
And attained that further extreme point
Where he found pleasure in hurting her,
He could not have told if he had tried;
But the pitiful thing concerning their life
Was that, as they stood over the little plant,
Marge was using all her diplomacy
On the man life had taught her to loathe,
In her fight to save the euphorbia.
Jacob was sparing the mat of rusty red
When it hurt him to miss the chance to hurt Marge
By grinding it to pulp with his heavy heel,
Because in his soul he really feared
That he might be the one to be stricken.
They had been warned to be careful about snakes
And the menacing, big, long-haired, black spiders.

So for that day he spared the euphorbia
With the virtuous resolve in his mind
That as soon as he could find another,
He would show Marge; he certainly would show her.
He had been showing her for twenty-five years;
He had shown her so exhaustively
That she had gradually reached the point
Where her greatest interest in life
Lay in the bright, rejoicing plant at her feet.

With almost equal yearning she was brooding
Above the earth shielding the roots she had set,
For there were places where, in only a few days,
She could see tiny, pink and green heads coming.
Her heart expanded and quivered over them;
Her soul hourly throbbed in high exultation

That her careful work had been effective.
She had been the means of saving the lives
Of the loveliest things she ever had seen.

Mingled with the strange uplift in her heart,
Nauseating waves of pure dread swept her.
When Jacob saw the flowers, what would he do?
She looked at the ridiculous gate and posts
Fulfilling the demands of his inner light.
If she could endure to see those grotesque things,
To use them gravely on going to the road,
Why not have her hedge of exquisite color
If she chose to do the work to produce it?

Because these things happened in Sunland
After the beneficence of water,
The dinner-horn and blue-curls raced sun and moon
To thrust their attractions upon Jacob.
Having seen the perfect, luring flower forms,
Marge could easily visualize her hedge;
On either side it would soon be waist-high —
A woolly, pinkish-blue mist on the right hand,
Having clusters of green needles like pines;
And on the left, a bloody-red challenge
Of equal height and exquisite foliage;
While, as on the desert, humming, song-wingéd birds
Like brilliant, flying flowers would tread air
As they tip-tongued each nectar-filled, red horn.

Marge watched her dear wildlings tremulously,
Surreptitiously she carried water to all of them,
No matter how strenuous the day's work,
Then cunningly kicked sand over the wet soil
To conceal the evidence of her misdeed.
She worked long hours at clearing the desert,
Quite as hard and efficiently as Jacob;
She was busy morning and evening cooking,
Sodden at night from physical exhaustion.

Then a shocking thing came to Marge's notice.
Grubbing resisting, parallel swathes all day,
She and Jacob had striven with the desert,
Matching the strength of their wire-muscled arms
Against the strength of its myriad branches,
The grappling depth of its interlaced roots.
Precisely when she began watching Jacob
She did not recall in studied after-thought,
But two realizations persisted:

Disagreeable as Jacob long had been,
He was becoming so very much worse
That Marge felt there must be consequences;
Some outside agency was responsible.
She shrewdly suspected that the nightly trips
Jacob made to the corner fruit-stands below
Had much to do with changing conditions.
He had always drunk when with drinking men;
He never had been intoxicated,
Never had really neglected his work,
Nor had he formed a demanding appetite.
Now he was drinking wickedly-brewed poison
Until ominous results darkly threatened.

Marge realized that Jacob was not well.
As she watched, the surprising conviction came
That she was almost, if not quite, the stronger.
She watched him circling a manzanita,
Rare in color as the euphorbia,
Very similar in its maroon shadings.

Had Marge not learned the futility of appeal
During years of experience with Jacob,
She would have asked him to spare the little tree.
They had space for more fruit and vegetables
Than their combined strength could cultivate.
The shapely manzanita was so lovely,
She felt a conviction nearing certainly

That it would bear appealing flower clusters;
That it might produce luscious fruit of value;
That to destroy such beauty without knowing
For what purpose the good God had evolved it,
Would be not far short of desecration.

Since life had forced Marge to become what she was,
She set her lips and continued her work.
She shrank as Jacob slashed the larger branches,
Circled the roots deeply, and grasped the trunk,
Pushing, pulling, throwing his weight forward,
Bending himself backward, kicking, heaving,
First using the axe, next the sharp mattock,
Still unable to uproot the sturdy tree
Even with the aid of prolific cursing.

Marge never knew exactly why she did it,
But when Jacob dropped the mattock, wiped his brow,
And stepped a few yards away to get the axe,
She left the greasewood with which she was wrestling,
Laid steady hands upon the manzanita,
And called upon her utmost strength for aid.
When Jacob turned, to his intense amazement
He saw the stump yielding, the roots lifting.
The task he had not been able to perform
Accomplished before his eyes by his wife
Without her showing undue exertion.

In following natural impulses, at times,
Marge had done some extremely unwise things.
Never had she done a thing so very unwise
As when she uprooted the manzanita.
Slowly there sank into Jacob's stubborn brain
The fact that he had dissipated his strength,
That he had poisoned his system speedily,
Until Marge was stronger at that hour than he.
Then quickly followed the nauseating thought
That she knew it and was proudly giving proof.

Jacob felt a surge of blind, bloody anger
That, if she did know, as she had proved,
She had dared to let him see that she knew.
The only reason he did not attack her
Was because she had picked up the mattock.
She had just shown that she was the stronger.
If she had had the hardihood so to provoke him,
It was possible that if he struck her,
She would defend herself convincingly.
In his soul Jacob was the same coward
As is every man who fashions his life,
Who shapes his years, who plans, for self alone;
Who makes of his union with a woman
The thing that he had made of his life with Marge.

At the supper hour slowly he followed her.
He was amazed at the yeasty hatred
That he felt germinating in his heart.
In the short walk, with the swiftness of thought,
He reviewed life from the day of his marriage.
Every defeat and chagrin he had endured
In all those years of unvarying failure
Flamed hot in his aroused consciousness,
Scorching his blood and brain to madness.

He looked at Marge's graying, wind-blown hair
Pulled in strands by the rebellious desert,
At her shapeless figure grotesquely clothed,
Her heavy, dragging feet in the clumping boots.
There surged in his heart an impulse to strike her.
That impulse had never before possessed him;
He had sworn at her as he had at his beasts,
He constantly did things to irritate her,
He studied out ways to hurt her feelings;
But to cause her physical suffering
Was a new thought that he grimly fostered.

He ate his supper in chill silence
Then left at once for the corners below
Where he drank that peculiarly vicious brew
Known to its reckless consumers as "white mule."
The maker of Jacob's nightly beverage
Had been more daringly unscrupulous
Than the average of illegal brewers.
The stuff Jacob drank avidly was poison;
It almost burned the lining from his stomach
And nearly maddened him with a fierce thirst
He had not known with any previous drink.

When he had gone, Marge sat on the veranda
And looked a long time at the euphorbia.
Over the barren stretch of sandy, pale soil
It spread like a rare, silken tapestry
Woven on the loom of the Great Artisan
In a creative hour of inspiration.
As Marge's eyes traveled from it toward the road,
She caught her breath sharply and gripped her hands.
From the gate-posts to the corners of the yard
She could see a tender forest of green shoots:
Such is the wondrous power of Sunland soil
In glad combination with spade and water.

Marge felt the first throb of exultation
That her soul had been allowed to know
Since the day that the first one of her babies
Had lived long enough to tug at her breast
And clasp a clinging hand around her finger;
In less than an hour she had lost the baby.

She looked at the upspringing, silver heads,
Exquisite in delicate pastel shadings
Of the humming-birds' particular flower,
Reinforced with red larkspur and fuchsia.
On the south side, growing in competition,

Were the rose-lavender, wool-wrapped blue-curls,
And the aspiring, mauve-misted thistle-sage.

A flame of excitement burned in Marge's eyes,
Her breath came short as if she had been running;
She leaned forward, staring in exultation.
She had greatly hoped, but this was assurance.
That tender, green line pushing up sturdily
Gave her all the proof necessary.
In one season of continuous growth
The shoots would harden and spring to a hedge
Fence-high and of color so exquisite
That not even the older homes of Sunland
Would have anything so arrestingly beautiful.

Then, with the swiftness of inner vision,
Came the blasting memory of Jacob.
Marge desired those flowers enough to dig them,
To stagger home under the heavy load,
To spade the deep trench in which she had placed them;
And she had freely used of the water
To coax them into loving their environment.
Not that water was scarce; Sunland had plenty
By installing hydrants where they were needed.
Water was changing desert into orchards,
Into vegetable and flower gardens,
Into homes knowing every comfort.

Marge sat staring at the line of the blue-curls,
At the frost-green of the humming-birds' flower—
Confident, happy, little heads breaking earth,
Eager for loving welcome by their savior,
Hastening to demand it from her.
A wave of nausea swept her being.

It was not wasted emotion on her part.
The next morning, on the way to the gate,
Jacob discovered the aspiring wildlings.

He stood glowering at them in amazement.
He followed the line where the earth had been turned.
He even noticed that water had been used,
Then concealing dry sand kicked over it.

The grin that spread over Jacob's lined face
Might have been mistaken by an observer
For delight in a pleasing discovery,
But any one looking in the depth of his eyes
Could have seen springing into life there
A tiny spark of malice, needle pointed.
He had not been so well pleased in a long time.
He had just discovered an unique way
In which he could further annoy and hurt Marge.

It would be foolish to kill the euphorbia,
Because, as she sensibly suggested,
He might be the one to need it first;
But this stuff was not medicinal.
He waited until he knew she would see him.
Then, for the first time since contriving the gate,
Instead of using the absurd contraption
He took a diagonal cut to the road
And with deliberation stepped crushingly
Where the humming-bird heads sprang the rankest.

Unconsciously Marge's hand flew to her heart;
A choking surge of anger strained her throat.
She looked after Jacob's retreating figure,
And for the first time in her experience
She tried to visualize to herself
Exactly how deeply she loathed a man
Who would make of the living of his life
What Jacob L. Travers had made of his.

She stood thinking about the men she had met
On the uncounted miles of her harsh journey
Between drear Kennebunk and Sunland orchards.

Many had none of Jacob's schooling in youth,
Had been no less buffeted on the journey,
And yet they had made some degree of success.
They had kept the respect of their families;
Many of them were living in modest comfort;
Some of them were rejoicing in middle life
In a depth of love surpassing that of youth.

After that, Jacob avoided the gate.
At each entrance and exit from his doorway
He crushed blue-curls or humming-birds' flower.

One day Marge followed him down the walk,
Her argument well thought out before she spoke.
"Jacob," she said, "why, in the name of sense,
Do you spoil the hedge I worked so hard to set?
When you wanted a gate, you should remember,
I helped you set posts and find timber for it."

She wanted to say that people in passing
Had laughed over the uncouth gate and posts
When there was no sign of a fence anywhere,
But to the last resource of her fagged brain,
To the deepest impulse of her robbed heart,
She was fighting to protect her flowers;
She was striving to be diplomatic.

"You made the gate," she argued earnestly.
"Don't you think it will look much better
To have a fence to the corner on each side?
If we should want to sell the place at any time,
The nicer it looked, the more you would get."

"Well, this is the place I don't sell," said Jacob.
"I like it here, and I've decided to stay.
I like the clean air and being full fed.
I like living where there's folks to visit with,

Places to go and things to do evenings;
We'll stay here and see what we can make of it."

"That is what I thought," said Marge eagerly.
"That was why I tried to help out your gate
By making a fence for it to open through.
If you would only keep on using the gate
And let those things be, as everything grows here
They would be fence-high before the season's past,
While prettier flowers you never saw."

Jacob listened, maliciously delighted.
"You made a fence to match my gate?" he said.
"Did it for love of me, did you? Well, thank you!"
Marge heard unbelievingly, yet with hope.
Following his thanks, Jacob approached the hedge
Not diagonally, but straightly.
Then he followed down the hopeful line of it,
Crushing each visible shoot with shuffling boots.

Then surged in Marge's heart a desire to strike him,
To hurt him physically, as he hurt her
With pain that was more difficult to endure
Than an injury to her seasoned body.

Marge sank down on the edge of the small porch,
Leaning her head against the side of the house.
An aching stringency cramped her pulsing throat;
Big, bitter salt tears squeezed from her outraged eyes.
She looked at the line of Jacob's footprints;
They had sunk deeply in the moist, sandy soil;
The humming-bird and fuchsia hedge was ruined.

He was heading toward the corner fruit-stands
Where other men like him gathered each evening,
Where white mule was dispensed to the daring
Who were willing to pay a high price for it.

It was certain as sunrise that next morning
He would destroy her blue-curls and thistle-sage
On his way to work in the desert clearing.

Marge was driven from her stolid repression.
All that had fallen to her lot she had borne
For the most part silently and tearlessly.
In that cruel minute she heard her voice crying:
"No, no! O God, don't let him kill my blue-curls!
Save, oh, save the beautiful thistle for me!"

In dazed wonderment she caught her hands together,
Staring as if she hoped to see a vision.
She had cried out in a passion of agony.
For the first time in her sorely tortured life
She had called upon the Lord, begging for help:
She had asked of Him a specific thing.
She stared uncomprehendingly before her
Where stretched the unbroken line of the desert.

Slowly she turned to watch Jacob from sight.
He should have been at work, since it was morning;
They should have gone together to the clearing.
She had scented the odors of drink on him;
Now she felt that this new horror was hers,
She tried to think when or how it had begun.

Jacob's energy had been to his credit.
He worked faithfully and desperately hard.
He drove himself, his beasts, and Marge without mercy.
He failed because he did not know how to plan.
He would not be advised by men who knew;
When he ventured into a strange location,
No one knew enough to teach him anything.

Marge did not know the hour that night at which
He stumbled into their uninviting room
And stretched his abused body beside hers.

She only knew that when his breath reached her,
It was with dry heat that was fairly withering.
She felt that she could produce a blue flame
If she held a lighted match to his nostrils.

The next morning he drank many cups of coffee.
He muttered that he was too sick to work,
And started around the house toward the road.
His way passed the exuberant euphorbia;
He noticed that the earth was damp around it.
He balanced himself on his left foot, surely;
He swung the right in a wide, forceful curve
That caught the plant on the toe of his boot,
Neatly shearing it level with the ground
And landing it on one of the gate posts.

He had intended, the next time he left home,
To trample the length of the other hedge row;
But the euphorbia draped on the gate post,
Its lovely, maroon sprays glistening with white
Like a decoration of delicate beauty,
Challenged him to finish his job properly.
Jacob advanced on the red creeper, cursing.

He caught it in his hand, as he passed the gate,
And started toward the fruit-stands, crumpling it.
He stooped and, picking up a small, flat stone,
Wrapped the euphorbia around it tightly
And hurled it far into the desert, full force.
Then he went to the insidious white mule.

Marge finished her work and stood hesitant.
Should she go on with the clearing by herself,
Or should she prove to Jacob conclusively
That she would not attempt field work alone?
Clearing the desert was man's oldest task;
She should have her time for her house and garden.

Marge studied the living-room appraisingly
To see if there were anything that she could do,
In an effort to make her barren house
More like the homes of the women around her,
That would not meet the same fate at Jacob's hands
That had befallen the humming-birds' flower.
If she had owned lace, she would not have dared
To hem and drape it over a window:
Jacob would have torn it down to wipe his boots.

Drearily she wandered through the harsh house,
Then going to the front porch she sat down.
At once the bare spot where the red mat had lain
Blighted her vision and arrested her heart.
The cry that arose in her throat was muffled,
But it was something very fearful to hear;
It began like the cry of a small, hurt child,
Ending like the snarl of a trapped wildcat.

That cry was the breaking up of endurance;
The euphorbia throve on a just excuse.
Marge believed that in case it was needed
It was sure salvation, as Lucy had said.
She was certain that Jacob thought the same thing,
And yet, merely to hurt and annoy her,
He would chance the dire risk of destroying it.

Just then her name came straining to her ears
In a voice that she failed to recognize.
Far away, a piercing, wailing utterance,
It came in hackled strands across the desert
Through the thickest of its thorny fastnesses
Where the yucca was armored the sharpest,
As if it had broken against the mountains
And threaded in ragged fringes through space — "Marge!"

There was none to call on her save Jacob.
Without thought Marge instantly sprang to her feet;

She ran down the walk and across the road,
Heading in the direction of the sound.
The bushes held her back; the thorns punished her;
The needles and spines had no mercy;
But in answer to the weird call of her name
She hurried on as fast as possible.

Then she came upon Jacob—a new Jacob.
He was lurching toward her with hands upraised,
Hoarsely calling for her in utter panic,
Begging for help in a scorched, terrified voice,
Until he stumbled and fell at her feet.
From his appearance Marge was certain
That he had fallen many times before.
She lifted him, crying, "Jacob, what ails you?"

He stared at her helplessly, like a stranger.
He had filled his system with all the white mule
They dared allow a man to have at one time.
As it burned its way into his thirsty veins,
He remembered his intention to hurt Marge.
When the dispensers refused him more drink,
He undertook a short cut through the desert.
He intended to unshackle restraint,
To unloose the evil passion in his heart;
He decided to go home and to beat Marge.

As he hurried through the restraining desert
Snatching at him with millions of angry barbs,
He was trying to determine in his mind
Whether it would be best to strike Marge
Or kick her or choke her or use a club.
He remembered her throat, firm and white and sweet,
At the time he loved to bury his face in it.
He thought of it now, lean, brown, and stringy.
He could vision no great pleasure in that hour
In sinking his itching fingers into it;
He thought it best to use his doubled fists.

Just as he arrived at that decision
He thrust his foot under a scrub-oak root
And pitched face-down in thick, protesting desert.
Distinctly he heard the low, humming buzz;
On his face he felt the needle-pointed fangs
Of that snake which carries death in its mouth.

He jerked back his head, rolling twice over,
Before he stumbled to his unsteady feet.
Instantly his sick and terrified soul
Sent up its first despairing cry for Marge.
He lifted his hand to his blood-stained face.
He started to run, screaming insanely.
He fell repeatedly, at last before Marge.

Stooping, she helped him to regain his feet.
She put her arm around him, bracing him,
And making what haste she could in the desert.
She guided him among rejoiced entanglements.
As they came to the open she paused for breath.
"Jacob, what happened to you?" she begged.

"I fell. Rattler struck my face," he panted.
"Take my knife and cut deep each side the bite—
And then get the euphorbia! Hurry, quick!"

Marge dropped her hands from his offensive body,
Facing Jacob L. Travers like grievous Fate.
It was plain that he was in extremity:
His puffing face was livid, his lips purple.
The exertion of running in the heat,
The insidious poison working in his blood,
The dishevelment of his punishment,
The dust he had encountered in falling,
Combined to make him a repellent object.

"'Get the euphorbia?'" she cried in scorn.
"Get it yourself! It is you who need it!"

Then Jacob remembered what had tortured him
Ever since he had started to rush to Marge
To have her apply the saving remedy.
The agony that twisted his ghastly face
Moved Marge to compassion; she caught his arm.

"Think! Think quick!" she cried to him imploringly.
"You haven't a minute to lose, you know!
It must be applied now! Where did you put it?"

Jacob hurried stumblingly across the road;
Again he plunged into the thickest desert.
Marge followed, trying to keep him from falling.
He stared around, bending to peer closely,
But his fear-blinded eyes failed to serve him.
He did not know where he had thrown the plant
That he believed would work his salvation.

A deep surge of fear shook and twisted him
As the poisons in his overheated blood
Rushed to his heart and then surged up to his brain.
Once again he fell, with feet drawn up,
And then slowly straightened out and rolled over.
A quivering shudder ran through his body;
He turned on his side and gasped wildly for breath;
Then he lay a motionless, silent figure.

Almost unconscious of what she was doing,
Marge snapped a tall alder spray beside her,
Sticking it deep in the sand and slanting it
So that it would shade Jacob's upturned face.
She reached behind her to untie her apron,
Spreading it over him so that the sky, the birds,
And even God, should He chance to look down,
Might not offend His eyes with such a sight.

Turning, she ran to the nearest neighbor's.
Lucy Martin had finished her morning work

And, freshly dressed, sat on her veranda.
When she saw Marge's flying figure coming,
She realized that something had gone wrong.

Whenever she had strolled down to visit Marge
With the hope of becoming friendly with her,
Marge had seemed childishly eager to see her,
But not once had she paid a return visit.
Lucy thought that the reason Marge would not come
Was because she was ashamed of her coarse clothes,
And, greatly fearing she had no others,
Had made a point of doing all the going.

Lucy was on the road calling for Henry
By the time Marge came in speaking distance.
He dropped his hoe and came to them instantly;
Together they ran down the road beside Marge.
In that short time Jacob could be located
By big, red-necked, wide-winged, sooty birds
Circling lower and lower over him.

Marge and Henry lifted Jacob L. Travers,
Carrying him across the road to the porch.
Henry bent over Jacob and felt his heart;
Then he slowly shook his head as he faced Marge.

"It's no use, Mrs. Travers," he said solemnly.
"I think he's gone. The rattler sure got him.
We should have left him right where we found him;
That's the exact wording of the law in this state.
The coroner won't like our moving him;
I'll have to go and call him up right away.
In case an accident like this happens,
He must come and swear everybody
And decide just how the man was killed."

Marge sat on the steps, gazing at the desert.
Lucy Martin crowded close, supporting her,
And laid a soft hand over Marge's gnarled ones.

She had not a notion what she should say.
From what she had seen and what she had heard
When the Travers clearing neared the Martin home,
She had been quickly convinced that her neighbor
Could not truly regret that her man was dead.
So she sat near Marge in wordless sympathy,
Trying her best to brace her physically.

Henry went to telephone the coroner.
While they waited, he asked what had happened;
It would help Marge before the officer
If she first detailed the occurrence to them,
Which was a thought of kindness on Henry's part.

He had other kind thoughts while they were alone:
He sent Lucy and Marge to brew some strong tea;
In their absence he emptied Jacob's pockets,
Taking the belt he found to save for Marge.

Presently Marge stood with her right hand raised
And swore to tell the truth as far as she could,
Also to the fact that she was without funds.

So the coroner took Jacob with him
To fulfill the requirements of the law,
To be meted the mercy of the county.
Henry Martin cranked his car and followed;
Marge and Lucy awaited his return.
The sun was dropping behind the mountains,
The desert was throwing lean tiger shadows,
When he came back to the nerve-racked women.

He sat down and looked at them inquiringly.
He hoped to learn from Lucy's attitude
And from Marge's strained, noncommittal face
The depth of grief possessing her veiled heart.
What he saw did not give him the feeling
That Marge was a deeply bereaved woman.

He had been actuated by the thought
That he must go carefully, be consoling.
Marge's set face and her cold, tearless eyes
Were shocking to Henry's sense of propriety.
It seemed to him little short of indecent
That she was not shedding even one tear.

At that instant Marge's wandering gaze
Chanced on the blue-curls and the thistle-sage.
She lifted her head. A peculiar thought-wave
Slowly crept over her incredulous face.
"My God!" softly breathed Marge's dazed mentality,
"If that's the way You answer a body's prayer,
Then praying is mighty dangerous—"
A slow, grim smile twitched her pallid lips.

Watching her, Henry saw the warring muscles.
He was an honest man, a capable man,
He had been searching Marge's strained face keenly
In order to feel his way, to be kind.
To him that smile was illuminating;
He had not imagined that his neighbor
Was a congenial man with whom to live.
He had not thought Marge a sheltered woman.
He had often said to Lucy in private
That he believed their neighbor was a big brute.
Why should a woman weep, when her heart was glad?

Henry leaned from his chair, speaking soberly:
"Girls," he said, "the big joke is on Jacob L.
There wasn't any rattler poison in his veins.
If he heard anything, it was a bumble-bee
Or the low-singing wings of a humming-bird.
If he was struck in the face by anything sharp,
It was some cactus needles when he stumbled.
There were some little marks that bled a trifle,
But he was not snake-bit any more than I am.
He died from an overdose of vile white mule,

Running in the hot sun to top it off,
And fear when he couldn't find the euphorbia."

Marge turned her head and slowly questioned Henry:
"Are you perfectly sure he is really dead?"

Henry took his time to consider that,
He critically studied Marge an instant.
He thought sweepingly, but of many diverse things.
"Yes," he said tersely, "Jacob L. is dead!
He's so dead he's in many different pieces,
You needn't worry your head any about that.
He won't come back to home in Sunland any more."

Marge's breath of relief was deep and strong.
After that they knew it would not be worth while
To offer condolence they did not feel;
They need not even pretend to be sorry.

They insisted upon taking her with them,
But she steadfastly refused their kindness.
Then they offered to remain all night with her,
But she persisted in being left alone.

"I know that it will be horrible," she said,
"But I shall get a grip on it in the start.
I have been mortally afraid of Jacob;
I shall not keep it up when he's dead.
I will spend the night watching the moon and stars,
In making friends with the comforting mountains,
And listening to what the desert says to me.
A mocking-bird built in the pepper tree,
Even though it is only a little one;
Her mate sang all last night mighty close here."

So Henry gave what was in Jacob's pockets,
And the belt, with due explanations, to Marge.
Then he and Lucy drove home to do their work.

They had much to review, to talk over,
But neither of them had unkind thoughts of Marge.
When they went to bed, Lucy crept close to Henry.
"Hold me tight," she said with a nervous shiver.
"I can just see him, and I am scared purple.
I don't know how Marge endures staying alone."

Henry gathered the little, pink bundle close:
"Shut your eyes and forget it now," he said.
"I was kind of riled with Marge in the start.
It didn't seem decent, the way she acted;
But since I studied her a little more,
I see she would be a blooming hypocrite
To try to pretend she was truly sorry.
If she did, we wouldn't either one like her
As well as we do when she is plain honest."

Part III

In the days that followed Jacob's passing
Henry and Lucy were puzzled about Marge
More than they had been at the beginning.
She did not tell them what sum she had found
When she examined the soft, leather belt
That she had seen since leaving Arizona
Across Jacob's back as he bent to his work,
And had felt at night still encircling him
When he lay in drugged lethargy beside her.

It had been a sharp shock, but gratifying.
She had shut her lips in scornful disdain,
Repeatedly counting the notes to make sure.
To Marge that worn, greasy belt spelled affluence.
She dressed herself in the very best she had,
Climbed on the first motor stage passing through Sunland,
And visited a store in Los Angeles.

The next time Lucy went down to chat with Marge,
She found two rocking chairs on the front porch,

A rug and more chairs in the living-room,
A new bed with clean, attractive bedding,
A small gas stove, whole cooking utensils,
And brightly-flowered dishes in the kitchen.

In a little, white cage on the front porch
A gold canary chirped to rosy finches
That came across the road from the desert.
In a becoming dress and easy, low shoes,
Her hands and hair showing careful attention,
Marge was hemming white scrim window curtains.
It was all very plain, simple, and cheap,
But it was new, pretty, and convenient.
It was abiding wonder in Marge's heart;
She was delighted with her purchases.

The obvious thing that stunned Lucy past words
Was not that Marge had made things comfortable,
But that she did not continue clearing.
Marge showed no signs of any intention to work.
When Lucy told Henry about the changes,
They speculated on what Marge would do.

"I think likely," said Lucy soberly,
"That she is broke up worse than she will admit.
You can see that he had been good-looking once,
And maybe she loved him when she married him.
It must have been a perfectly awful shock
To have him go like that—no warning at all.
I'll never get over the way he looked.
Maybe it kind o' took the tuck out of her
Till she's got to rest and calm down a few days."

The next morning Henry brought to Lucy
A board on which was crudely dabbled in black:
"Two uncleared acres for sale today. Cash.
Inquire of owner at first house to right."
"Where did you get that?" cried Lucy in wonder.
"Pulled it up from where Marge had driven it.

No one sees this till we've talked with her first;
If she is going to sell those two acres,
We should have that much more to add to ours.
We can pay cash down for as much as she needs.
Let's go and talk it over with her right now."

Marge, placidly hemming curtains as they talked,
And looking decidedly pale and tired,
Listened closely to all their arguments
Then sold two acres of her land to Henry,
Half cash, half the rest in quarterly payments,
The other half in labor when needed.

Then Marge turned over the small square of pine
And achieved in upstanding, black letters:
"Good working team and stout wagon for sale.
Wanted, a good milch cow and Leghorn chickens."
That deal also was soon consummated,
Then, for security's sake, to avoid risk,
Marge made a trip to a Los Angeles bank
To start a small account with what remained
After paying for Jacob's final move.

Henry and Lucy were still badly puzzled,
For Marge, who had worked slavishly with Jacob,
Left to herself, scarcely worked at all.
She kept her house neat and clean, as became her;
Always she watered and weeded her garden.
Through the noon heat and for most of her time
She seemed to be lying on her davenport,
Eating nourishing food, pampering herself;
They were amazed over her course for many weeks.

One morning Lucy took her sewing basket
And went down to visit with Marge a while.
She had grown extremely fond of her neighbor,
While at times she had been vastly entertained
When Marge talked of her experiences,

The places in which she had sojourned with Jacob,
Or showed interest in questions of the day.
She seemed so eager for enlightenment
That Lucy began giving her their paper
After she and Henry had finished with it.

Lucy sat stitching on her bit of sewing;
Marge passed her, carrying the little gold bird.
"I just noticed, as I came in," said Lucy,
"That your crop of euphorbia is spreading."

"Yes," said Marge, "Jacob only sheared off the top.
It just came racing at once from the roots,
And the sand seemed to be full of fine seed;
There are little ones coming all around.
There's going to be a perfect, bright carpet,
And it's going to stay right where it is,
Till it covers the whole front yard with beauty."

She reached both arms full height to place the cage.
Lucy, in line with her, caught her breath sharply.
"My God, Marge! You ain't—?"
She stopped in baffled, white-lipped amazement.

Marge turned to her a grave, lean face of assent.
"I've been speculating," she said evenly,
"On how long it would take you to notice."

Lucy sprang up and ran to Marge impulsively,
Putting her arms around her to hold her tight.
"Oh, Marge," she cried, "I don't know what to say!
Are you glad or sorry? How do you feel?"

Marge passed Lucy and sat in a rocker;
She silently studied the euphorbia.
Then she looked at the luxuriant hedge,
Knee-high and growing thriftily each day—
On one side of the gate-posts gaily flourished

The blue-pink curls and the wool-clotted thistle,
Opposite the silver-red and the deep green
Of the humming-birds' flower and the fuchsias;
The gate she had used at once for tomato-racks.
Finally she drew a deep, quivering breath.

"Well, considering my luck," she said slowly,
"It would take nerve on my part to be *glad;*
But I have always had the ugly feeling
That if I had had the right kind of food,
Any care at all when I needed it most,
And hadn't been forced to work like a stoker
To the very last minute of endurance,
I *might* have brought some of them into life,
Though only God knows whether, if I had,
They would have been of any comfort to me.

"There's one thing I've resolved about this one:
It's going to have a perfectly fair chance.
It means, if I can give it birth alive,
That I have got something of my very own
To love, to live for, to work for, to love me.
If luck runs the same for me this final chance,
When I have had everything as I should,
I won't feel so bad about all the others.
I'm going to get some slight satisfaction
Whatever happens to me, when my hour comes."

"But what in this world will you do?" cried Lucy.
"I have got that all studied out," said Marge.
"I got some ideas from your newspapers.
I always have had plenty of warning;
I think there will be time for you and Henry
To take me to town. You will, won't you?"

"Why, of course we will!" exclaimed Lucy.
"And we'll tend the cow and the chickens for you,

And we'll take care of your house and garden—
Of course, we'll be glad to do anything we can."

"I have reckoned on your helping me," said Marge.
"Any day you happen to be driving to town,
If you don't mind, I'll ride along with you.
I am going to the County Hospital;
It isn't necessary to be a pauper;
I can pay for as good a room as I want,
But I don't need to pay more than I can afford.
I wrote them a letter asking everything.
Two women can divide the time of a nurse;
Even at that I will get the first real care
I ever had in my life at such a time,
And It should have an honest-to-goodness chance,
Which is something none of the others had."

"Are you making little things?" questioned Lucy.
Marge shook her head slowly, introspectively.
"No," she said. "If this one happens to live,
They will have what will be wanted at first.
If I can really keep this one with me,
There will be many long years ahead of us
To make the little things that it will need."

Lucy was divided between eagerness
To stay and help Marge plan for her future,
And a desire to reach Henry with the news.
Henry was as interested as his wife.
That same day he elaborated reasons
For driving to the city on business
In order to take Marge to the hospital.
When all her arrangements were perfected,
He took Marge and Lucy to see a picture
And bought them Eskimo pie for a treat.

When Marge stepped from the car at her home,
She laid her folded hands, almost human,

On the car door and looked straight into the eyes
Of Lucy, and then, even longer, of Henry.

"Do you folks ever pray?" she asked abruptly.
Henry fiddled with the steering gear for help;
Lucy answered promptly, "Of course I do."

"Well," said Marge, "I hoped that maybe you did.
Two may have much more influence than one.
Once I asked the Lord to do me a favor,
And He didn't waste any time answering.
I don't want to presume on that, of course;
I don't want to tire Him with importunings;
I have limited myself to *once* each day;
But I will be awfully glad, when you pray,
If you will ask for me to be shown the way
To do the right things in the time that remains,
So I won't be left with empty arms again."

"Sure I will," said Lucy in tremulous tones.
In confusion Henry started the car,
But when he slowed down for her at their front door,
As Lucy glanced at his face in stepping out,
She could see traces on his sunburned cheeks
Where tears of compassion had coursed their way.
Her own face was twisted with emotion.

"I guess you will pray, too," she hazarded.
"Yes, I guess I will," slowly answered Henry.

Many weeks later, Lucy, watching constantly,
Saw the preconcerted signal flying.
Henry had carefully kept the car ready;
In a few minutes they were speeding with Marge
Over the level, shining roads of Sunland,
Racing far past the limits of the law
On their way to the County Hospital.

In the reception room, waiting patiently,
For long, anxious hours they faced each other
Before the heartening message was brought
That there was a nine-pound boy, sound and strong.
Neither doctor nor nurses in careful search
Could discover the slightest trace of reason
Why he should not thrive as other babies.

Before they left, they tiptoed to Marge's bedside,
Her gaunt figure was outlined by the cover;
Her china-white face was pain-lined and distorted;
Her big, black eyes darkened the lids like shadows.
In deference to the nine that were lost
The thoughtful nurse had laid the living bundle
In Marge's arms to strengthen her assurance.
She was too weak to do anything more for them
Than to reach a hand and force a weary smile.
The nurse slipped down the enfolding blankets
To show a little, wrinkled, red, swollen face.

On the way home they were very silent.
They stopped at Marge's anxiously waiting house,
Where the gold bird clamorously welcomed them
With gusty trills and gushes of exultant song,
Then chirped lonesome inquiries for Marge.
They cared for the sleek cow and the chickens,
And then went home to attend to their own work.
That night, when they lay on their wakeful pillows,
Lucy said: "I am getting mighty anxious
To know exactly in what state Marge Travers
Is going to come out of this mentally.
Is she going to think she got that baby
By all of us praying in concert for it,
Or is she going to have the common sense
To see that she got it in such good shape
Merely by taking decent care of herself?"

"She is a sensible woman," said Henry.
"I think she will feel it's a combination.
One thing I know: I wish to heaven we had
A nice, fine boy like that of our own."
"'Nice!'" sneered Lucy antagonistically.
"He looked exactly like a skinned rabbit."
"All right," said Henry, "you just wait six months
And see what you will say about him then."

Two full weeks Marge remained at the hospital.
All that time she lay perfectly passive,
Doing whatever she was told by her nurse.
The sensations of being bathed, brushed, massaged,
Were such pleasant, unique experiences
That she was so strongly tempted she begged
To prolong her stay for another week;
But her room was needed, so she had to go.

During those days of thrilling experience
In being the mother of a family,
Marge's brain was unduly stimulated.
Each time her son, a warm, mouthing miracle,
Lay tugging at her unaccustomed breasts,
She endured the sharp pain without flinching;
But her eager eyes searched him minutely
For any first faint sign, any indication
Of pain that might be unendurable.

She importuned each nurse who entered her room
For the most accurate information
Concerning colic, care of colds and teething,
And all the other ills of babyhood.
She agonized over bumps in learning to walk
And grew tremulous over mumps and measles.

She dreamed of the Los Angeles high school
And began considering colleges.
All too soon she faced the dreaded question,

"Why do you never talk about my father?"
She had a picture of Jacob at his best,
Taken for her before they had been married.
His face was handsome, his clothing timely,
She knew exactly where to lay hands on it.

She could talk indefinitely of Ohio;
From there she would skim lightly to Sunland.
She could never know that Jacob lost his life
Taking a short cut on his way to beat her.

One day Marge justified her fine fiber
And reinforced the good-looking picture
By naming her son Jacob L. Travers, Junior.

Because of her diet, rest, and infinite care,
She was nursing the finely-growing baby.
When Lucy and Henry came to take her home,
They were dazed at the change in her appearance.
The tan had faded from her neglected face,
Her hands looked like the hands of a woman,
Her hair had been brushed into beautiful waves
That coiled becomingly around her head.
Her nurse had done the shopping she required,
So there was a little package for Junior.

Lucy insisted on holding the bundle,
So suggestive of castile and boracic;
She said Marge was so weak she might drop it.
As Marge passed between the crooked pepper posts,
She stretched a hand to her hedge on either side,
As if she were giving blessed greeting,
And paused to look down at the euphorbia.

Her knees and elbows were shaking crazily,
Partly through weakness, partly through vague fear
Of what life with her son might develop.
She had bought Holt's book on the care of babies,

She had made a list of the things she must do.
In the bundle with the baby's outfit
Was a little emergency kit for her
That might be required for his necessities.

She was frightened almost past self-control,
But she used all the common sense she had.
She would have liked to sit in the rocking-chair
Holding the baby in her arms all day,
And to lie with him on her breast all night;
But the nurse had said that would be bad for him,
So with real fortitude, heroic courage,
She handled the small, enchanting body
Only when bathing and nursing it by rule.

The remainder of his healthful babyhood
Jacob L., Junior, lay in a clothes-basket
On a pillow, blanket covered, in the open,
Turned from side to side occasionally,
Given the required amount of water,
And his mouth was always swabbed after nursing.
He was not a colicky baby, not cross.

By the time he had accomplished three months,
Marge had come to believe that he would live.
When he had thriven splendidly for six months,
Came the placidity of assurance.
When he had passed his first birthday, one year old,
And sat confidently in his high-chair,
Drumming with a spoon, kicking with lusty feet,
And forming his mouth in the shape of words,
He was a king on an undisputed throne.

Before him knelt three adoring subjects:
Marge, wearing the shining crown of mothers;
Lucy, slowly allowing his sweetness,
The beauty of his body, his gold-spun hair,
Waving above brown eyes and pink cheeks,

To take possession of her uncertain heart,
Each day breeding the envy of desire,
Bringing her soul closer capitulation.

Henry was frank in worshipful devotion;
He carried Junior on the road, to the desert,
Showed him the birds, the flowers, the mountains;
And worked overtime and too hard on Marge's land
In order that she might have more time indoors
For the real and fancied needs of Junior.

As she tended her baby's body each day,
Always Marge quested for signs of her future.
Gazing intently into his lovely face
Like flawless, finely-cut, pink cameo,
She constantly searched, felt and probed deeply
With the discerning fingers of her soul,
For indications that would presage the way
To the long-sought land of heart-ease for her.

Once, after a glorious romp with Junior
In which he knock-mauled Lucy with chubby fists,
Pulled her hair, and plastered her with wet kisses,
She raised to Marge an anxious, quivering face.

"Marge," she asked softly, "is it so awful bad?"
Marge understood. She went to her neighbor,
Only a soft little girl after all,
When compared with her years of experience,
And put her arms around her protectively.

"Lucy," she said, "I have weathered it nine times
With no preparation and scarcely any care,
And once again with all the care I needed,
And I equal any woman of my age yet.
I won't lie to you. There is pain, of course.
It can't be avoided, but it can be borne.

"With any one as young and strong as you are,
With the constant care that would surround you,
With the way Henry would love and pamper you,
It wouldn't be like what I have gone through;
And no one could tell you what it would mean
If you had in your arms a boy like Junior
That had been born through your love for Henry.
Isn't it worth trying, little neighbor?"

Lucy bowed her dubious, young, yellow head
For prolonged hair pulling and pommeling.
When she lifted her face to Marge at last,
It was lighted with the glow of high resolve;
A long struggle had immolated self.
"Yes, I believe it is," she assented.
"I'll tell Henry. He'll be the gladdest man!"

When Jacob L. Travers, Junior, attained two,
Marge took him to the children's department
Of one of the big stores of Los Angeles
And set him on the counter to keep him near.
She was asking for blue gingham by the yard
To make aprons for his play where she worked.
The clerks promptly succumbed to Junior's charms,
Never having seen a lovelier baby.

"You don't want," said a pretty saleswoman,
"To bother him with petticoats and aprons
And all that old-fashioned, restricting stuff.
Why don't you get little, ready-made rompers
And save your time for something truly worth while?
It really doesn't pay you to make things,
Children can creep and walk better in rompers.
Let me show you how much freedom they give."

Then she proceeded to pull off the apron,
Putting Junior into an attractive pair
Of crinkly, peach-blow colored, crêpe rompers,
Working transformation fairly enchanting.

Marge made a flashing mental inventory
Of the state of the garden and orchard,
The crops she was growing on her three acres.
She thought of the contented, full-uddered cow,
Her gracious partner in the business of life,
From which she was selling milk to neighbors.
She thought of her thrifty, scale-free young orchard,
By the grace of Sunland heat and water
Reaching a state presaging fruitfulness.
She thought of the remainder of the contents
Of Jacob's miserly-guarded loin belt,
Still lying untouched in the bank for safety.
She thought of her body, seasoned and limbered,
Stronger than it had been during past hardships,
Because of nourishing, appetizing food,
Only a fair amount of daily work,
And the elimination from her life
Of the killing strain of annoyance and fear.

Then she looked at Junior appraisingly.
The clerk was stacking more peach-blow beside him
And shaking out pale blues with narrow, white bands.
The mental review had been quite sufficient.
Marge succumbed without a whimper of protest.
The clerk said there should be white-ribbed stockings
And white-topped shoes to wear with the rompers;
Marge promptly laid in a generous supply.

Then she went to her clean, refurbished home,
Feeling the heart-expanding exultation
Of again having done something she pleased
Merely because she found pleasure in it.
She bathed Junior to wild-rose-leaf sweetness,
Brushed his curls to spun sunshine silkiness.
She tried first the blue, then the pink on him,
But peach-blow won enthusiastically.
They started on their way to show the Martins.
As they reached the walk, Jacob L., Junior,
Released his tight grip on his mother's fingers,

Balanced a second on his unsure young legs,
His attention attracted to the ground.
He sat down, leaning over the euphorbia
Spreading abroad two years of glowing color.

In white consternation Marge studied him,
Her face slowly growing lined and ghastly.
He leaned closer above the delicate flower,
His strong, irresponsible hands stretched out.
Marge's mouth suddenly became parched and bitter;
She opened her lips, but no protest issued.
Junior looked closely at the euphorbia.

He was seeing the spreading, maroon-red stems,
The delicate, white-banded, pink flowers,
The rich, unusual green, heart-shaped leaves
Narrowly margined with white and shaded with brown.
Marge's hands gripped together unconsciously,
Pressing hard against her soul-sick body;
Almost a repulsed look swept into her eyes.
Tensely she watched Jacob L. Travers, Junior,
Awaiting the quality of his impulse,
That nothing could have induced her to divert.

The little hands hovered uncertainly,
Then, with a determined movement, they lowered
Until they touched the mat of euphorbia.
Junior lifted a face of discovery:
"Pitty 'lower!" he cried in smiling confidence,
"See, Munner, such a pitty, pitty 'lower!"

That instant the carpet of euphorbia
Became to Marge a sacred prayer rug.
She suddenly collapsed in the midst of it,
Dropping her redeemed head in Junior's pink lap.
His straying, unconscious hands of innocence,
Lightly caressing the safe euphorbia,

Were also driving from his mother's heart
The bitterness of constant misgivings,
Flooding her singing soul for all time to come
With adoration which is akin to worship.

(*The End*)

"Field o' My Dreams"

An idealized description of a part of the Limberlost North property at Sylvan Lake in northeastern Indiana, "Field o' My Dreams" first appeared in *Outdoor America* 3 (December 1924): 26–27. *Outdoor America* is published by the Izaak Walton League of America, of which Porter was a founding member. The poem has the following headnote: "When the Izaak Walton League was yet in its infancy, Gene Stratton-Porter, because of her great love of the out of doors, rallied to our standard and has remained one of us, lending priceless support through her gifted pen and charming personality." The stone "sentinel" owls still stand on the gateposts at the old entrance to the site.

FIELD O' MY DREAMS

There's a green alluring meadow, where in happy dreams I wander,
Drawn by its enchanting beauty—each night drawn to linger in it,
With a triple cord of strong strands, spun of shining silver longing,
Strands of haunting beauty, subtle fragrance and spontaneous song.

On the north my field is bounded by a stretch of untouched forest,
Carpeted with early wild flowers, hardy, cold-defying snow boys,
White and blue and yellow violets, pink Canadian and bird's-foot.
Later, burns the torch of foxfire, shine the stars of sparkling campion.
Here the stately trees of lakeshore rise from moist soil, deep and fertile,

Always beckoning with high hands, signaling the distant heavens;
Good fellows, joyously mingling, never tiring of their places.
All day leaning to give greetings, profferring kindly reassurance;
All day singing, keeping silence; all night whispering to each other.
Giant oaks, red, white, and chestnut, straight as ship masts home together.
Cloud veiled elms, wild cherries graceful, maples, coffee trees and lindens,
Big gray beeches, widely stretching arms alike to earth and sky,
An ancient blue ash, hale and hoary, gathering his young around him.
One decrepit old hackberry, highly topping all the others,
Deeply scarred with lashes given by the warring winds of ages.
In the cleft breast of the forest flame the holly and red elder,
Like ruby jewels flashing on the breast of a comely negress.
In its tangles of blackberry, in its overcreeping wild grape,
A bell-bird tells her beads of gold, tells them one by one, one by one.

On the east my field is bounded by a hollow, deep and olden,
Its lazy creeping bedstream, laughing loudly in its falling,
Chuckling over pebbly shoals, shouting round the stones resistant.
Spreading wide in pools fern bordered, shadowed deep by rose and cornel.
Here lift hoods of rank skunk-cabbage, leaves of green-gold freshly shining,
Through the seas of yellow cowslip, 'mong the buttercups hand painted.

Tall grow here the honeyed lindens, sycamores stately, wearing patches,
Aspens quake when air is breathless, dance mad rhapsodies in storm.
Between big, thirsty roots down-reaching, always creeping toward the
    waters.
Jack-in-his-pulpit preaches love, collects the gold of celandine.

On the south the open highway girds the globe and returns to me.
Here a close set hedge of buckthorne, shuts my field in from the roadway,
Reinforced by wild sweetbrier, pink dogwood, redbud and elder,
At their feet in wild abandon, lilies truant, cabbage roses.

Across the road in confused tangles, hawthorne white and bittersweet
Dodge the county supervisor, whose law strong hand dares take their lives.
On the west the hedge of buckthorne marches gaily to the forest,
Wearing robes of green, brocaded with small flowers of misty yellow,
Draped with frills of pale rose aster, and the filmy lace of beard-tongue,

Fringed with goldenrod so feathery, spiderwort and cerise paintbrush.
All its festoons deftly fastened with rosettes of frail sheep sorrel,
Jeweled on its breast and shoulders with the egg-filled nests of song-birds.

Leaving far a world of turmoil, my dream road slips through my gates.
Passes posts of snowy matrix, carries me by sweeping glaciers.
Stones thick-set with blood-red oblongs, stones with pebbles blue in color;
Stones commingling shades mosaic, in a thousand blends harmonious.
On each post a horned owl perches, a big bird of frowning aspect,
Guards with stony eyes of watching all my wealth of treasured wild flowers,
Warning in a voiceless language: "Who, who robs one flower of life,
Sins a sin that knows no pardon, against the God of all things growing!"
Past these sentinel posts my road, slowly winding homeward to me,
Creeps on through my field of visions, through my field of purple clover,
Guarded by its tall blue sailors, ever standing at attention,
Smiling on the bouncing Betties, sturdy, coy, they wave, pink-blushing,
Past the ravine of the aspens, past the orchard, old, pathetic,
Crowned each May in youthful promise, God's mystery of pink and white;
Then comes Fall's abject fruition—apples wormy, tough and blighted.
My road greets the nodding wild flowers, the tossing tree, loved by children
When it waves its emerald pennants on the lightest breeze of summer.
Then it runs into a valley where the face of earth smiles broadly,
Flickering from a bed of lilies, mixed with turtle head and saffron,
To its mate of fringed gentians, Oswego Tea and button bushes.
Now it rises from the valley, to the lake goes swiftly speeding,
Where the mirror of its surface, pictures clouds and magic forest,
On its heaving breast of silver—ever shifting blue quicksilver.

Then it parts the hedge of buckthorne, with its fragile wildflower border,
From the gutter-snipes adjoining, in the bed of fly-up-the-creeks,
Where commingle in profusion, flowers that flew the garden fence,
Coreopsis, larkspur, poppies, hollyhocks and ragged robins
And those other rowdy gamins, 'neath the footboard slyly creeping,
Striped grass and valley lilies, lovage, myrtle, daffodillies.
The road loves those close companions, gaily waves to them a greeting,
Then abruptly turns to leave them; lingering, it could not pass them,
Plunges in the wide-armed forest, down its cool and song-thrilled spaces.

Thus in dreams my field I wander, breathing of its far-flung fragrance,
Listening in ecstatic trembling, to the thicket catbird's medley,
To the sparrows of the hedgerow, to their cousins of the brown earth,
To the notes of robin redbreast, to the bluebirds of the orchard,
To its cooing doves and vireos, preaching in their lace trimmed pulpits,
In the apple-tree cathedrals, where our God most surely dwells.
Then I hear old Bob White calling, oven-birds in purple clover,
Nightly sing the larks on fence posts, dance the clownish bobolinks.
Black-eyed, bloody-coated redbirds, bold buccaneers send challenge gay,
Warblers in the cowslip thicket, ever roll glad fantasy.
This is where I go in dreamland—this the field in which I wander.

"Whitmore's Bull"

Published posthumously in *McCall's* 53 (June 1926): 8–9, 84, 102, 103), "Whitmore's Bull" conveys Porter's admiration of her parents and her nostalgia for the wild and domesticated flowers of her childhood. A lengthy headnote says that the poem "has the roll and tang of a saga—an early American saga of the time when our land was young and when the 'giants of those days' tamed the wilderness and made the prairies flower." The personal and family history it conveys is largely factual, although the Strattons made their journey from Pennsylvania to Indiana before Porter's birth. Her humor and detail regarding children, plants, animals, and insects represent Porter at the culmination of her poetic faculties.

WHITMORE'S BULL
Underneath, the floor of heaven was smoky blue-purple,
Joyous stars, like fireflies heliographing happy messages
Across the vast, rolling meadows of the sky,
Filled space with evanescent silver light.
A luminous mist of star dust veiled the Milky Way.
The big crystal moon-ball, raying tender beneficence,
Rolled its immemorial course in serene splendor;
In its light, Whitmore's Meadow had its hour of high Magic.
The big white monarch of the Pasture of Spring
Slept on a sweet bed of royal purple clover

Delicately brocaded with the blue of Venus'-looking-glass,
Intricately outlined with the gold of sheep sorrel,
Curtained with filmy white alder and blackberry,
The pink of wild rose and the red velvet of sumac.
When the Sky Decorator brushed the first broad stroke
Of orange-red across the canvas of the East
The bull arose, shook himself, lifted his head high,
And drove his breath through his nostrils
Like steam escaping from a powerful engine.

His back was a pole, his sides were far plains,
His breast a plateau, his neck a mountain,
His great head was nobly proportioned,
Having questing eyes and far reaching horns, finely polished;
His legs curled abruptly to shapely feet,
Each carefully fitted with twin shoes of ivory.
His milk white coat disclosed the rose of his skin.
Like curling flax the brush of his tapering tail
Swept the earth as he passed over it.
Strong waves of muscle rippled over his body
As he went down to the overflowing river
To thrust his cool, sweating nostrils
Into a still pool of muddy water.
The clay sucked loudly as his feet left it;
Turning, he climbed the bank to the meadow.
Before breaking his fast he lifted his head high,
Furrowing his neck in layers of deep folds,
And snorted menacingly at all creation.
A rod away, young Mistress Bob-o'-Lincoln
Slipped from her leaf-sheltered house
And wove her way among the clover stems
For a long winding distance of concealment
Before she took wing to tell her mate
That a strong wind blew and the earth shook,
Making her brooding heart fearful.
Nearer the white bull, a rattlesnake, curved to strike,
Felt strange trembling beneath him, knew fear,
And hurriedly sought secure shelter,

Among the stones heaped under a big white oak.
"Cowk! Cowk! Cowk!" screamed a lean turkey hen,
Vanishing from her nest of stippled eggs,
Sheltered by a fence corner berry thicket,
To the promised refuge of adjoining forest.

Catapulting from the tallest fence rider
On which he daily saluted the sun's red rising,
A frightened lark passed along the danger signal
Through a hasty utterance of his offertory, "Spring o' year!"
An adventuring wind, permeated with hawthorn and apple perfume,
Forced the stretch of meadow into green waves, purple crested.
The white bull closely searched his entire domain
With a penetrant look of intent deliberation.
Seeing nothing that in any way irritated him,
He snorted menacingly to intimidate the unseen;
Then dropped his muzzle to dew-wet grasses and clover tufts,
Here and there embittered to dandelion and daisy.

Crunching big mouthfuls, dragged up by the roots,
Grinding flower and fodder alike in his milling jaws,
The white bull slowly grazed his way across the meadow.
Once a plucky little ground sparrow refused to move,
Because her first egg had pipped against her mother heart,
Until a ruthless hoof drove her into the earth.
The steel-colored, red-lined, yellow-spotted wing of a moth
Clung for a long time to the slaver of his jaws.
At the far fence, the bull paused to survey the world.
Mr. Bob-o'-Lincoln on the closest fence rider
Rejoiced incoherently because his mate had escaped.
A brooding dove, with anxious, fear-filled eyes,
Crouched low on her nest, set flat on a fence rail,
Hoping she was hidden by sheltering sumac.
Far across country a cock crowed challengingly;
A cow insistently droned a mothering note.
It was not the urge call of reproduction,
But it served to remind the white bull
Of the irritating limitations of his kingdom.

In the culmination of his strength, hunger satisfied,
He felt the devastating lust of the wild,
The galling restriction of confinement,
The desire to dominate other living creatures.
He knew that he belonged in his meadow,
That his world was bounded with the strength
Of a nine-rail fence with heavily wired stake and rider;
But the odors of spring tormented his nostrils,
The ferment of domination was yeasty in his heart.
He set his determined breast against the fence,
Pushing until the rails began to yield and to slide.
He lowered his head, steadily pressing forward,
Repeatedly tossing upward and outward,
Until the rails scattered widely before him.
The dove's nest was torn to wind-driven fragments;
The broken bird, struggling to escape,
Beat the bull's face with her wings of gray satin.
Aroused, he cleared the fence, snorting in triumph.
Stepping proudly, in the heady exultation of liberty,
He entered a field of young corn, knee high.
He did not consider pausing to feed on its sweetness;
He was Nature obeying Nature's primal impulse.
He began pawing up the rounded hills of lush corn
And tossing it over his back as he advanced,
Rumbling a low, far echoing bellow of menace,
To inform the world that Might was abroad
Seeking weakness that could be conquered.

He pushed down snake fences as kindling wood barriers,
Soon accepting the invitation of the traveled highway.
The first farm house he passed, a watch dog raved at him,
Leaping at his head, snapping at his legs and nose,
Flashing under and over him, harrassingly acrobatic,
So that he whirled in helpless bewilderment,
Not understanding that his great body hampered him
In facing this small, agile thing of torment.
When he could endure the punishment no longer
He turned and ran until his blood flowed hotly.

At the next house, warned by his threatening advance,
The children stoned him from the vantage of a shed roof
Until he again fled from these mites of irritation
He was amazed to find himself unable to evade.
Then a farmer passing in a buggy on his way to town,
Striped the bull's side in long welts with a whip,
Trying to persuade him to return to his home.
The bewildered white bull began to heave and to sweat,
To drool in long streams from his heavy jaws,
To see red challenge every way he looked;
Yet stubbornly he continued his infuriated advance.

Pawing up the wayside grasses of a fence corner,
He trespassed on a nest of busy yellow-jackets.
Enraged, they swarmed over his head in reprisal,
Stinging his nose, his ears, his neck, his gullet,
With many infuriating electric needles.
The white bull tore his head through the bushes,
Rubbed it against his sides, tossed it high in air;
A mad thing, he ran amuck down the dusty open road.
His hoarse bellowing sounded a mile ahead of him.
He charged at a high embankment in passing,
Viciously biting out mouthfuls of the overhanging clay
Which mingled in dirty drippings to the earth
With the slaver oozing from his foaming jaws.
My Father was working at a pair of trestles beside the road
Where I was handing pickets to him,
When the white bull came threateningly toward us.

Father was not large, but he was large enough.
His forehead was high, his mouth wide,
His eyes a steady steel-blue in color.
His hair was fine, dark, and slightly wavy.
The contour of his face was sharply chiseled,
While on his high, defiant cheek bones
There burned always the unfading flush
Of the roast-beef red of old England.
His legs were firm as arch supports to a bridge.

His back was broad like Atlas' in the mythology book,
Big skeins of living whipcord were his muscles.
He was a beautiful figure of virile manhood.
He had walked beside the plodding ox-team
That brought us all the way through the wilderness
When of traveled roads there were none,
As we came prospecting from Pennsylvania.
With only an axe he had once killed a bear
That had climbed on the roof of our cabin
And was trying to come down our fireplace.
With his confident hands, he had choked the rabid dog
That came foaming and panting among us children.
He had been forced to match his unarmed strength
With many an Indian in earlier days of travel,
And with one violently insane neighbor
Who had a mattock to his advantage.
He could carry twenty stone dead weight,
And lift one end of any beam at a barn raising.

That morning he was building a new garden fence
Which he hoped to complete as a unique gift
For my mother's coming birthday celebration.
Carefully, one green laden panel at a time,
He took down the old fence of split clapboards,
Set new posts, sawed at the lumber mills,
Mortised in long, stout cross pieces,
And nailed on them exactly spaced, neatly pointed pickets.
The panel he had taken down that morning
Was the one beside the cinnamon pink bed.
Of all the world of flowers in her garden
Mother best loved the spicy cinnamon pinks.
That is much to say, for hers was an enchanted garden,
Everywhere it proved that it was a work of Magic,
For she had the Gift of Flowers from her Creator.
For thirty years she had yearned with unabating love
Over the growing of each plant in her garden,
And daily she worked the miracle of love
Into the lives of each of her flowers.

Anywhere she saw a plant she had not,
She never hesitated to suggest to a friend:
"Only a little bit of a slip, please,"
Or, "Just a wee pinch of that rare seed!"
Then she cut the slip diagonally, topped it,
Stuck the lower end in a raw potato,
And planted it, sheltered by a cabbage leaf,
With exactly enough water in fine soil.
Or she wrapped the bottom of the cutting in cotton,
Put it in a wide-necked bottle of rainwater,
And hung it in a warm, shady place,
Very near to the shining of the sun.
Sometimes she rooted her slips in wet sand,
Protected from the air by panes of glass,
And no plant ever had been known to droop,
Under her well-considered, loving ministry.

After many years, her garden became a Magic Garden,
Having a fence shouldering running trumpet creeper,
Honeysuckle, morning glories, and cypress,
Screened by japonica and sweet scented shrub,
Flowering almond, and feathery, red-berried asparagus,
And cabbage, moss, blush, and radiant roses.
You can see why Father had to use extreme care
About working out the posts and panels
And fitting in the new fence through the vines.
A Bartlett pear tree reached its wide white arms
Protectingly across one side of her garden,
And an ancient May cherry tree guarded the other;
There was a catalpa flowering in one corner,
And a white berried privet filled another.
An old sweet briar grew in a third corner,
While a Morello tree, mysterious with pale bloom,
Shaded the corner where Father and I worked.

Wide boxed beds lined the fence on its four sides.
From them, in the days of earliest spring,
There winked a drift of star petaled flowers

Like a little Milky Way fallen into our garden.
Sky blue bells rang their music to the bees,
While in bowls lined with unsalted clover butter
Mother extracted their perfume for her linen chests.
There were gold daffydillies, white Easter flowers,
Long rows of brazen tulips, red and yellow.
Later, this bed, like exquisitely appliquéd velvet,
Draped from the top of the fence row to the earth.
Tallest stood sunflowers high above our heads,
Ever beckoning pink lady-fingers suggested courtesies,
Tall hollyhocks and dahlias of many colors,
Blue foxgloves and darkly freckled tiger lilies.

Now one panel of her garden fence was open.
Ramping down the road toward it,
Came Whitmore's big white bull, enraged;
His jaws frothing strings of dirty slaver
That trailed the dust in bubbling festoons.
He saw my Father busy at his work,
Beyond him the opening to the Magic Garden.
No doubt the man and the loaded work trusses
Seemed small obstacles to the adventuring bull.
Very likely he scented our barn beside the lane,
And the presence of cattle in our pastures,
So he came straight toward us in slow progress,
And the blue-green, blushing, cinnamon pink bed.

It was May in the life of the garden
And May in the whole world—late May.
I had heard all those Indian and bear stories
From ruffled, starched pinafores onward.
Now I stood undaunted beside my Father
Waiting to be told whether I should run.
The bull paused before us, lifted his head, and snorted,
Snorted until he blew a drift from his nostrils
Across my Father's blue chambray shirt sleeve.
Then the bull lowered his head and advanced,
Each forefoot alternately pawing the dust

Until it flew higher than our heads.
My Father had a stack of pickets before him,
Evenly laid, carefully tapped into place,
All ready for the four-square pointing.
He held them firmly with his knee,
While the oiled saw shone in his hand.
When the bull thrust his horns toward the trusses
To toss them from the line of his advance,
His nose touched the grass at our feet.
"You would, would you?" asked my Father,
"And right through Mother's cinnamon pink bed?"

He dropped his saw, snatched up his hammer,
And leaning over, he deftly tapped the bull
Near the base of one long angry horn.
Close behind the ear Father tapped him—
Such a little easy tap—
Nothing like the knock-maul stroke he used
To drive a wedge into a felled tree.
I noticed that, and I particularly noticed
That his voice was low and steady,
While his feet seemed to be set on earth
As firmly as the big mulberry pie tree,
Standing in the center of the field across the road.
Such a little tap!—

The white bull slowly sank on his knees
With one retching bellow of anguish,
Boring his nose in the grass of the wayside.
Even his thick hind legs wavered back and forth
As if they, too, would fail to bear his weight.
Then my Father leaped over the loaded trusses,
Caught the tail of the bull and began twisting it—
Twisting the tail of the mighty bull!
At every twist Father drew back and pulled hard.
All that we had heard of boastful conquest before
Was as nothing compared with the roaring
When the tail of the bull was pulled while twisted.

The tears ran from his eyes, he chilled.
The sweat washed down his dust sprinkled sides,
While he staggered to his feet slowly,
Abjectly imploring mercy he had not deserved.

Then my Father kicked the white bull forcefully;
Kicked with all the strength of his body,
Merely to insinuate to the King of the Pasture
That it was high time for him to be returning
To his grass, his clover, his daisies and his river,
To his annoying fence with its wired stake and rider.
The bull started slowly up the road toward Steeles',
Because his wavering legs bent like drawn bows.
To our wood-yard gate Father followed the bull,
At every step administering punishment,
While at each twist the big creature bellowed loudly
And gathered momentum as he proceeded.

Father was running in long, flying strides,
Landing so forcefully on his feet
That he slapped up the dust in small clouds
When he released the amazed monarch.
Father had to run on for quite a distance
And then slow down gradually to a walk,
To keep himself from falling headlong.
He was laughing and breathing in short gusts
When he came back to where I was standing,
Picked up his saw, and went on pointing the pickets.
"I'll wager a pretty His Imperial Majesty
Comes not this way again in many a day," he said.

Silently I gazed at my Father.
Then I looked up the pink and white walled road
Hourly beckoning to each seeker of conquests,
And watched the bull turning Steeles' corner.
He was traveling at a wabbling drag-trot,
Hugging the fence closely for protection,
Still of threatening voice, raising no dust,

His dry tongue hanging far from his mouth,
While his huge head seemed as if it were so heavy
That never again could he exultantly lift it.
Sick, dirt-encrusted, beaten and abject,
He was hurrying to the safety of his meadow.

I sat down on a stack of pickets, until I was needed,
And thought deeply about my Father;
Then I thought even longer about Whitmore's bull.

The Unpublished Poems

Some years after the 1971 death of Gene Stratton-Porter's daughter, Jeannette Porter Meehan, Deborah Dahlke-Scott, who had written an article on Porter for *The Smithsonian,* told me that Porter's grandson, John Meehan, had some of Porter's papers and that she had copies of them.[1] He graciously gave me permission to ask Ms. Dahlke to copy hers for me. They include letters, journal entries, page proofs, galleys, and some poems in typescript and manuscript, among other papers.

The page proofs, dated 1920, include a title page for a book, "A Collection of Poems by Gene Stratton-Porter."[2] The proofs appear neatly polished, nearly ready to be printed, although they include no table of contents or page numbers. Another group of papers, galleys of poems, were probably intended for a book titled "I Live Again. [3] A letter from Mrs. Meehan indicates that she was preparing such a book in the 1930s.[4] The galleys bear the notations "Set up for Surf, Publishers" and "By Order of Hale Horton." No information regarding Surf, Publishers or Hale Horton has been located. The poems in these galleys are in very rough form, needing considerable editing.

Both the page proofs and the galleys include poems previously published in magazines and over twenty others that seem never to have appeared in print. Exhaustive research indicates that neither the book represented by the page proofs nor the one from the galleys reached actual production. Among the same papers, copies of most of the poems in the page proofs and the galleys also occur in typescript, manuscript, or both. In addition, there are typescripts of a few more poems that do not seem to have been prepared for publication of any kind.[5]

In transcribing these poems, I have made some editorial decisions, choosing between different versions of the same poem, selecting punctuation and stanza divisions where they have not been entirely clear, and so forth. In attempting to preserve Porter's intentions, I take full responsibility for any errors I may have committed in interpreting the available signals.

John and his brother James Meehan, and Monica Berg, James's daughter, have kindly given their permission to publish these poems and to include the other poems that have also been previously published. These include the poems that Porter placed with magazines and in George Ade's *An Invitation to You and Your Folks from Jim and Some More of the Home Folks*, all of Porter's poems in *Music of the Wild* and *Morning Face*, as well as the complete texts of *The Fire Bird* and *Jesus of the Emerald*. Therefore, all of Porter's known poetry can appear together, for the first time, in one volume.

This is the kind of discovery a scholar longs to make, and it has compelled me to bring the poems to publication in combination with the rest of her poetry, both for the pleasure of Porter's many longtime readers and for more recent scholars to see the full range of Porter's work. I remain deeply grateful to all of those who have helped make them available in this form.

A few comments on the poems might be helpful. The narrative in the poem, "The Quest for 'Three Birds'" appears to be based on fact. Porter tells the same story in a longer, prose article, "The Search for Three Birds," which appeared in both *Good Housekeeping* and *Tales You Won't Believe*.[6] The essay gives a fuller framework and tells the story in greater detail.

In an undated letter to her friend, Dr. Charles Wharton Stork, after she had moved to California, Porter wrote that, although she lacked confidence in her poetry, she had nevertheless continued to write it throughout her life. She regretted that "when I did write anything, for the greater part it met the fate of 'The Wine Pitcher,' which is still awaiting its day after nearly twenty years."[7] One typescript bears the date 1904.

"Pacoima's Answer" exists in typescript and galley form, the former in three variants, each with emendations. There and in typed and handwritten tables of contents, it has a total of six different titles: "Pacoima's Answer," "The Canyon's River," "Pacoima," "Pacoima's Waters," "Pacoima's Canyon Waters," and "Pacoima's Racing Waters." I have selected both text and title as the ones likeliest to reflect Porter's intentions.

"Cymbals" and "For a Young Girl's Autograph Album" appear not to have been prepared for publication.

PROMISES

Peep o'day, you flood my lake
　　With a blood-red splendour.
Peep o'day, you tint my flowers,
　　With a rose-light, tender.
Peep o'day, you seek my woods
　　The glad promise bringing
That I may have another hour
　　For working and for singing.

High o'noon, you gild my trees
　　With a pure light golden.
High o'noon, you warm my heart,
　　With deep purpose olden.
High o'noon, you bring to me
　　Daily bath of re-creation,
Promising my heart and soul,
　　Something nearing inspiration.

Light o'moon, you gently creep
　　To my window casement.
Light o'moon, your radiance turns
　　To fairyland my dark emplacement.
Light o'moon, you steal to me
　　Soft as night birds' flying,
Promising your furling wings,
　　Bear me love undying.

THE QUEST FOR "THREE BIRDS"

For years I saw it in my books,
　　A graceful plant and slender,
The perching place of three flower birds,
　　Upon a frail stem tender.

For years I searched the valleys through,
　　The forests' dank recesses,
I hunted where maidenhair
　　Shakes out her wavy tresses.

I searched through every swamp I knew,
　　And every cool green highland,
And many a day I watched for it,
　　When crossing Kestler's Island.

Then one tired day on my home road,
　　A country woman hailed me—
A woman that I truly loved,
　　Her kindness never failed me.

"Come see the rarest flower," she said.
　　"To us it is a stranger;
The children ventured in the swamp,
　　Where it is full of danger."

I followed her into a house,
　　Past groups of kindly neighbours,
Wondering why they were not at home,
　　Busy with harvest labours.

She led me to a darkened room,
　　And with a brown hand tender,
Lifted a scarf of webby lace,
　　To show what service she could render.

Upon a pillow in unwaking sleep,
　　My heart was hard to master—
There lay a tiny perfect thing,
　　God carved from purest alabaster.

"It did not die," she gently said,
　　"For it had never breathed;

But name for me these lovely flowers,
    That I have round it wreathed."

And there, with wings of wild rose tint,
    Nested round a still-born child,
"Three birds! Nodding Pogonia!" I cried:
    My eyes were wet, but my heart smiled.

THE BELLS I HEAR

In the grey of dawning, I hear the sun-bell ring,
Its first stroke wakes cock-robin, so he begins to sing.
The coot in mist-cloaked marshes makes baritone reply,
The forest gobbler gobbles, peering from half-shut eye.
All nature greets the sun-bell, with an answering note.
Back it pours a clamour, from its brazen throat;
For the sun-bell is a big bell, ringing over sea and wold,
When dazzling sunlight ribbons each morning are unrolled.
For the sun-bell is a big bell, gold wrought, of purest yellow,
Its clapper is a glittering globe, striking rich notes mellow.
It wakes the field and forest, it wakes the drowsy city,
It wakes the traveled ocean, it wakes us without pity;
Around the world each day it rings, its age-old journey hasting,
Admonishing with far-flung voice: "Good Folk, it's time you're wasting!"

Early in the evening the silver moon-bell flings
Its sweet-toned notes of calling to myriad folded wings.
Nervous little brown bat, night hawk and whippoorwill,
Go hunting when it wakes them, empty crops to fill.
To men of sunny labour, it sounds their call to rest,
To men of nightly labour, it says: "Now work your best!"
To pilferer and jailbird: "I'm marking time on you!"
To man and maid sweet-hearting: "Now has your hour come true!"
The moon-bell is a burnished bell, cast from silver pure,
With shining pear-shaped clapper, striking clear and sure.
Nightly I hear it ringing, when the moon lifts her face pale,
And loans the world the splendour of her cobweb silver veil;
While on this kindly Magic, adoring watch we're keeping,
The moon-bell slyly warns us: "Good Folk, you should be sleeping!"

The sky-bell is a joy bell, blown from crystal blue,
All day it rings its measure, it chimes all night for you.
A slender oval clapper, busy on its azure wall,
The tired world loves to answer such a cheery call.
The flowers like happy faces, bluebell and harebell ring,
Half-mad with mating ecstasy, the birds begin to sing.
Deep in stony passes, the snake coils round his mate,
Deep in wildwood thicket the red deer stamps, elate.
The sky-bell rings a miracle, in the heart of man and maid:
"Come, dance and sing, and love! Never be afraid!"
The sky-bell tones its music over sea and land,
It sets the world on tip-toe, a carefree, singing band.
It echoes the voice of laughter; of love a sure decoy,
It peals the invitation: "Good Folk, come dance for joy!"

Another bell I often hear, a deep arresting note,
The big, bronze sea-bell, with urgency in its throat.
In ocean's farthest cavern, where the mermen dwell,
The mermaids love to polish their fins on the rim of the bell.
The merbabies shoot the shoots, down its slippery round,
Or shouting cling to the clapper, trying to muffle the sound.
Through the waves its stern voice carries the width of the world,
Straight to each waiting mortal, but once its call is hurled.
I sometimes hear its stroke nearby, the passing of friends I see.
Some day it will be clanging the message that waits for me;
For the sea-bell is the final bell that mortals ever hear,
Some of us listen smiling, some in white-livered fear,
For when it tolls a summons to you, from the cavern in deep sea,
Its certain voice is calling: "Good Folk, come to eternity!"

MAGIC
    Sweet, make Magic with your hair,
Let teasing Southwinds set the snare;
Fair as flax-skein, moleskin fine,
Veil these asking eyes of mine,
With its clinging mesh divine,
    Sweet, make Magic with your hair!

Sweet, make magic with your eyes,
In their deeps your secret lies,
Flies when timid lashes lift,
And screened glances, winging swift,
Swoon my soul in love adrift;
    Sweet, make Magic with your eyes!

Sweet, make Magic with your lips,
Red as rose Lineata sips,
Dips to quaff and floats away;
O my Sweetheart, I would stay!
Make of this a holy day,
    Sweet, make Magic with your lips!

Sweet, make Magic with your breast,
Take my head on it to rest,
Drest in honeyed loquat spray;
For this mercy hear me pray,
Take my heart to keep for aye,
    Sweet, make Magic with your breast!

FOR YOU!

There's a colour miracle in my head, of evanescent hue,
Like brilliant flower faces, that pearl moon-rays subdue,
    Oh, how I'd love to give this wondrous gift to you!

A flower homes inside my head, of pure fringed gentian blue,
It grows the best for poor folk, warmed with sun, watered with dew,
    Oh, how I'd love to set one beside your door for you!

There's a Magic Jewel in my head, with rainbows stealing through,
Such teasing, dancing radiance, breast of woman never knew,
    Oh, I'd know joy unmeasured, if I could give it you!

The bird that sings inside my head, sky-feathers in cloudland grew,
It whistles a cheery flute-note that courage will imbue,
    Oh, I daily wish that I might share this buoyant song with you!

And in my head there is a vision, a gift God gives to few,
I see the whole world loving, unselfish, gentle: born anew—
Oh, I would gladly give my life, to make that vision true,
For You!

THE WINE OF LIFE PITCHER
Life sought the great Master Potter, crying:
"Mould me a pitcher, O Potter!
With the water of the sacred Ganges,
Mix your finest red clay of Babylon,
Swing your wheel and surpass your most exquisite shapes.
With your rarest minerals of crimson, green and purple,
And your finest leaf of pure gold,
Decorate it as you have embellished no other.
Light your fires and burn me a glaze that will never tarnish.
Encrust it with carbuncle, diamond, sapphire, emerald and jasper.
In all ways make my pitcher the rarest ever moulded,
For from it, I shall pour the Wine of Life,
Into the hearts of humanity's embryonic children."

Joyed of this task was the great Master Potter.
His face absorbed, his eager fingers trembling, he stooped,
And lovingly lifted the fine red clay of Babylon.

Cried Life to the Potter:
"Divide my pitcher into four separate wine cells!
From one, let me pour to the children of good fortune,
The white wine of Joy,
Brewed from the white grapes of Persia,
The white mulberry of Palestine,
And sweet with the honey-dripping blossoms of the locust.

"Let me pour to the children of misfortune,
The stringent green wine of discontent,
Brewed from the sour wild grapes of Greece,
The bitter berries of the oil tree,
And bitten with the tang of rue and of wormwood.

"To the children of self-sacrifice and honour,
Let me pour the rich red wine of love,
Pressed from the ruby grapes of Italy,
The blood-red pomegranates of Egypt,
And tinctured with the intoxicating delights
Of the crimson poppies of Cathay.

"And into the hearts of the children of harlots,
Hypocrites and murderers, let me pour the black wine of death,
Distilled from the black fruit of the fox-grape,
The stringent colocynth apples of Gilgal,
And deadly with the touch of hemlock and vervain."

Cried the great Master Potter:
"Nay, Life! Only one wine cell can I mould in your pitcher!"

He covered his face and sat bowed beside his wheel,
While Life turned away with slow step, exceedingly thoughtful.

Next day came Life with hopeful face and hurrying footsteps, crying:
"O Potter! All of my wines have I emptied into two great vats!
Mould me a pitcher of only two wine cells,
That from one, I may pour to the children of gladness,
The white wine of Joy;
And from the other, to the children of sadness,
The purple wine of sorrow!"

Slowly the Master Potter shook his head,
And with finality he made answer:
"Only one wine cell can I mould in your pitcher!"

The third day came Life,
With a face like the radiance of love,
While his feet like homing swallows crossed the mountains,
From the distance he shouted in exultation:
"Mix your clay and swing your wheel, O Potter!
Into one great vat have I emptied all of my wine.
Mould me the pitcher with only one wine cell,

That from it I may pour
Into the hearts of humanity's new born children,
The Common Wine of Life,
In mixed proportions of Joy and of Sorrow!"

·To his willing wheel sprang the great Master Potter.
With skillful hands he lifted the fine red clay of Babylon,
While the glory of his face, dimmed the sunshine all around him.

OUR LORD'S CANDLES
There is a gossamer flame on the desert,
    There is radiance on the scarred mountain face,
Where our dear Lord sets His candles,
    On green altars high, and sere treeless space.

His candlesticks are living steel bayonets,
    His waxen tapers are tall and mast-straight,
High flicker the flame tongues of whiteness,
    Lighting the night for souls wandering late.

Where hungering lions roar on the mountains,
    Where gaunt coyotes yap in the sage,
Where the aloof and tormented desert
    Pours on the wayfarer its parching rage —

There the great heart of enduring mercy
    Lifts high a flame that is mellow as foam,
To show the lost how our Lord loved them,
    When He loaned His candles, to light their way home.

"OLD WALT"
Every slender, shining leaf of grass,
Keeping undaunted pace with winding, footworn roads,
Becomes an eager, warring blade uplifted for Democracy,
    Because of him.

Every freshening, salty breeze of ocean
Or clover-perfumed breath of inland field

Makes priceless wine of heady vintage,
  Because of him.

Every ruminant herd in pasture lush and tender
Lifts eyes of placid self-containment,
And gives me heartening greeting as I pass,
In signs I learned more intimately to translate
  Because of him.

When I follow the open road, combing its bordering grasses,
With eager, exploring fingers, in long continued daily search
For the twinkle of gold star grass, the blue of Selkirk's violet;
Scanning marshy snake fences for some vine long sought in wild estate,
Some rare, infrequent creeper like Dutchman's pipe or climbing boneset,
Watching higher for the lace of coffee tree or fringe of Chionanthus;
Ever as I go, before me always marches an heroic figure,
Deep breathing, eagle-eyed, sometimes with deliberate, absorbent step,
Sometimes outdistancing the rush of frenzied gale,
A figure compelling, justly self-denominated Immortal,
With clouds and sky, grass, flowers, birds and animals,
Beggars, labourers, rich men, school-mistress or free companion,
A motley company, each eagerly companioning him for one little hour;
Whitman ever marches down the road ahead of me.
Happy I, content to follow, working patiently in his shadow,
Ever loving earth and sky, man and animal, with deeper devotion,
Striving to do cleaner-cut, more faithful work,
  Because of him.

PACOIMA'S ANSWER
O Pacoima's eager waters
Race the gladdest that I know,
She skips, and leaps, and pirouettes,
In the down-rush of her flow.
She speeds in clouds of rainbow mist,
Like the tinted veil on morning's face.
She chants, and trills, and gurgles,
She shouts on her wild race.

She hustles through the deep pools
To madly rush slim passes,
Trips a Pixie dance, on pebbly shoals,
Like Spring impassioned lasses.
Adown her deep slashed canyon bed
She tones her ringing echo,
And gaily answering to its call
Darts the slender, graceful gecko.
She waves her foamy banners high
The blue sky's tender smile to greet,
She coquettes with proud-breasted walls
That guard her at their faithful feet.

She mats the sunshine's golden hair
In wild, gem-sprinkled tousle,
And flings a gush of amorous spray
To pet her love, the nesting ouzel.
In daring leap she leaves her bed,
Riding on witch winds highly flowing,
To broadcast cotyledon seed
In a rain of random sowing.

Her canyon walls of lace looped green
Smile down in serene splendor,
Waving with graceful, ferny hands,
High-heaped with kisses tender.
They lean to shield the laughing stream
Racing in ceaseless flurry,
While lovingly they call to her:
"O Pacoima! What's your hurry?"

And then Pacoima rocks in glee;
She takes a mad-cap, spray-crowned leap,
For well she knows a little child
Is tossing,—thirsty in its sleep.
Full well she knows an orange grove
Awaits her loving ministrations,
And many a broad potato field

Covets intimate relations.
Perhaps she knows her chance to wet
A courting mocking-bird's gay whistle,
Or slake the thirst of desert goats,
Browsing on sage and thistle.

Straight to the wee folk Pacoima runs,
Her canyon loves effacing,
Laughs to the breast that gave her birth:
"I lavish Life! That's why I'm racing!"

THE HEART OF THE WORLD
I am the heart of the world!

I am the heart of mercy,
Beating strong in the breast of the generous,
And the heart of the miser,
Housed in the tenement of greed.

I am the steady, dependable heart of love,
Enduring endless sacrifice uncomplainingly,
And the hot, leaping heart of passion,
Causing untold suffering.

I am the unselfish heart,
Beating only for my brothers,
And the heart of self-indulgence,
Worn pulseless in daily excesses.

I am the happy heart,
Leaping in the abiding place of joy,
And the heart of hate,
Strengthening the arm of murder.

I am the heart of innocence,
Firm-walled in the tender breast of the virgin,
And the far-wandering, wanton heart,
Swiftly driving the shriveled feet of the harlot.

I am the heart of the world!

Through my endlessly pulsing veins
Flows my blood of spendthrift and miser,
Philosopher and fool, lover and betrayer,
Samaritan and Levite, saviour and assassin.

I am the heart of the world!

Into my heart I dip my pen and write my confession.

ESCAPE
In green pastures of dim lake bed, beside bass-weed forest,
Big mouthed black bass, steel spined, alert, round eyed,
Snapped up tortured, sluggishly swimming minnow;
Shot his wild limit of line over muck bed and sand shoal,
Arose, smashing the sky-mirroring surface to spray,
A drawn bow, spat a broken barb into the sunlight—
    Escaped!

Cooing bird of grey satin, tender eyed and pink billed,
Daintily picking bits of scattered cheat and broken corn,
One coral foot over-stepping an innocent circle of horsehair;
Sky planing wings beating unconscious earth in wild terror,
Breast feathers rising in air in ultimate struggle,
Where it cut deepest, the strained hair parted—
    Escaped!

Savage black bear, blade-footed, hunger nosed,
Sniffing the canyon for ant house and bumble honey,
A bleating kid, quivering, frantic chained bait,
A mad hunger rush, a crash into a concealed pit,
Foaming mouthed battle against walls of sheer granite,
One wire rooted crevice of advantage—
    Escaped!

A life house of miraculous white bone framework,
Wired with red veins, muscle furnished, velvet carpeted,

A fair dwelling, past earth in delicate workmanship,
Flame scorched, wave tormented, blizzard bitten,
Helplessly rocking where tornado meets quicksand,
An open window, silent wings spiraling skyward—
    Escaped!

MY BEACH-COMBER
Where daring waves spray in silver delight,
Plumed with smoke feathers from the wings of night,
Oh, Love, scoop me deep, with the steel of your hands,
A homing bird's nest in earth's restless sands.
Weave me a blanket of gold primrose sweet,
Heap a blue drift-fire my coming to greet,

You are the wind of my deepest desire,
Your eager hands are my food and my fire;
You are the tang of pomegranates to me,
You are my mountain, my valley, my sea.
You are a beacon, in the tryst we keep,
Warm in your heart-house my wee dream birds sleep.

You are my Beach-comber, I am your nest;
I am your impulse, but you are my rest.
You are the thrush song my secret heart sings,
I am your nest, but you are my wings.
On these sure pinions, my soul takes its flight,
Beach-comber, light your blue watch-fire tonight!

DESIRE
    I am the heart of Desire!
Over the rose hills of dawn I come through the grey mists.
So swiftly I travel, my eager feet skim the dark mosses lightly.
To my streaming hair cling tender, gold-green leaves, dew-wet.
I seek the rich valleys; searching for the delights of youth.
My throbbing heart is ripe for the baptism of love.

    Are not the bees tumbling over the columbine?
    Do not the gold butterflies their flight entwine?

Are not bird bills locked on branch and vine?
See the swift hare waiting in her leafy shrine!

Of all nature, shall I alone hesitate before the Gates of Life?
Hear my voice, for into the valleys I come, calling—calling for my mate;
Calling out of Youth's springtime; calling with forceful insistence.
My hurrying feet shall not be stayed by langorous enchantments,
Of star flowers I will weave me a bridal wreath for my brow.
Of moonshine and cloud fabric, I will spin me shimmering vestments.
From high-lifted hands, I scatter broadcast delicate petals of snow
To make wedding garments for the lifting virgin flowers around me.
Each day I swiftly travel onward seeking my destiny.
        For I am the heart of desire!

FULFILLMENT
    I am the heart of fulfillment!
Through the valleys I wander, in the ripening days.
To my damp temples clings my heat-waved hair.
Contentment sleeps in my drowsy eyes, lulled by singing cricket and cicada.
In joy o'erflows my satisfied heart to nourish a quickening heart beneath it.
Around my feet in joyous abandon, tumble the fruits of my harvest.

    Low humming bees stagger in pollen laden flight,
    Silken cocoons shut great moths from sight,
    Bright birdlings feast and fly in delight,
    Young hares nibble purslane under cover of night.

I have known fulfillment and tasted life's supreme sweetness,
I have woven love's crimson poppies into a wreath for my hair,
In purple and gold I have draped me with rare pleasure,
I have drunk the wine of life from sparkling goblets of crystal.
From wide-spread hands, I sift gold pollen wherever my path leads me
Thus I impregnate every waiting flower form bordering my way.
Long, long let me linger in these happy, sheltering arms,
        For I am the heart of fulfillment!

APPREHENSION
    I am the heart of apprehension!
Dream haunted, I gather red leaves and late flowers of purple.

My lips have so long hungered; why am I deserted?
My hair is whitening, my hands shake over the flowers.
So long have I watched for my children, I cannot see clearly.
Can the hearts of Youth have carried them to the far gates of morning?
I too would return to the ecstasy of that short journey.
But my feet are irresistibly driven toward a lonely narrow valley.

Why are brown leaves o'er earth lightly spread?
Why do caterpillars burrow in earth a deep bed?
Why have the bright song birds all southward fled?
Why does the cold serpent lie as if dead?

Oh, I fear these gloomy days, this silent lonely valley!
Chill winds numb my frame, as they drive me before them.
They are the sower, whipping the black stalks to seeding.
I will help by scattering dry leaves to cover their rootlets.
But there is no one to shelter and warm my weary heart.
Long, long have I awaited the return of love.
Come back, oh come back, heart of o'erflowing joy!
My life-blood is chilled by dread fears unnamable.
For I am the heart of apprehension!

ABANDONMENT

I am the heart of abandonment!
Into the forest grey and white I flee from the savage winter.
I am driven before torturing blasts that chill and freeze me.
Gaunt terrors stalk among the bare trunks, and in my eyes are dark terrors.
Shriveled are red lip, firm breast and loving heart.
I have no strength to search farther for love and my children.

There is no warmth in the dry leaves around my feet.
The brown cocoon swings deeply coated with sleet.
Bats hang dormant in their cavern retreat.
Where my wood brothers hibernate no winter winds beat.

Sleeping securely all nature awaits the quickening touch of renewal.
With aching hands I gather snowflakes and pile the white fleece higher
To make seeds and roots safer in their cold beds.
But for me there is neither shelter nor sleep of oblivion.

For I am the heart of abandonment, shivering alone before my Creator.
This creeping cold in my heart will soon still my pulses forever.
Oh God, I pray thee, let me also awake in the Springtime
To travel again the glorious green highway of youth.

    For I am the heart of abandonment.

OX-HEART CHERRIES

They blazed colour over the stall of the Japanese vendor,
Like cabochons nested in frilling of gold lace,
Like pigeon blood rubies on the fingers of courtesans;
Cherries walled with fresh leaves, three inch stem lengths,
Heart shaped, colour arresting, packed in orderly rows,
Materialized blossoms from white orchards of San Diego,
Sun molten to blackish, fruity red, palate tormenting,
Placarded in forbidding broad brush strokes, "40¢."

Each lemon and grape fruit, each orange and apricot,
Deepened in tint from proximity with the cherry box.
The gold bananas were large borrowers from contrast,
Their red cousins discovered that they were not red;
The pomegranates turned their most brilliant cheeks,
To learn that they had left real colour in Hebron.
Pastel pineapples stood in bayonetted ranks on the top row—
Cherries, from the land of the Conquistadores,
Flaunting their lure on the streets of the plethoric city,
Crying: "Behold what God hath wrought for your pleasure,
From hot sand, blue sky, sun gold and running water!"

Came a small brown maid of the blood of Spain,
Her little fist clutching a penny for the spending.
As a butterfly her soul responded to the magic of colour;
Her red mouth watered over luscious temptations.
At each finger pointing the oiled Jap frowned negation;
Until the full lips quivered, the asking eyes misted.
Then the racing feet of desire, skipping here and there,
Swiftly tip-toed over the edge of the inviting cherry box.
Big eyes promptly exulted in clamorous certitude;
The immobile Jap dropped the penny in a cash register,

The eager eyed little maid whirled feather lightly,
Dancing to the castanets she dangled above her
Three ox-heart cherries from the orchards of San Diego.

OH LORD, — LADY!
After crossing the ford above Escondido,
The aspiring road circling the mountain shoulders
Billows through green scrub oak and purple sage thickets
Like a delicate scarf of wind-looped buff chiffon;
Like the braid pinned for the work of a lace-maker,
When weaving its intricacies into flowers.
Sometimes the single track pirouettes in fantasy,
Again it rolls up in sweeping curves of beauty,
Always it dances onward from height to greater height
As it seeks the high source of the singing Rincon.

Going to Sky-land, on the right hand, one false step
A sprawling plunge among rocks and manzanita,
Luck if not a sheer sweep to ultimate silence;
On the left hand, overhanging heights of menace,
Slanting walls of flower painted invitation,
Big rosettes of frosty, blue-green cotyledon,
Rock leek, freely proffering thirst quenching coolness,
The curling maidenhair, fronds of ravelled fern fringe,
Lupin, white, rose purple, deep blue or fady pink;
Ruby, salmon and yellow monkey flower faces,
Slender shaggy spires of red or dark blue larkspur,
Cocky little roosters with faces brown and yellow,
Pride of California tossing purple plumes
Over every shrub and ancient rock face.

Heading toward the Rincon, walked a fine Lady,
Pert traveling suit of mauve, fine feathered head-gear,
Rocking heels, flaxen hair, grey-blue eyes of glamour,
Hiding far in the depths of their deep welled secrets
Shone a steel light, needle pointed, sharp and stinging,
Lips having long acquaintance with life's laughing weather,
The hall-mark of experience set plainly on her,
On this day, "seeing sights" her manifest mission.

Slender hands of flower whiteness carried loosely
Volatile leaves of forbidding green-gold menace,
White tasseled flowers, drooping, pungent, sickly.
From a whole world flaunting flaming invitation,
She had gathered seeping serum, water blisters,
She had gathered days of torture, nights of anguish.
From a world steeped in luring flower attar,
From a world gaily singing deep notes of colour,
She had chosen poison oak— *Oh Lord, Lady!*

THE MISER

Save an amber ray of sunshine
    For the close of your career,
Keep one song of all you're singing
    For Life, when it grows austere.

Nurse a spark of inspiration
    For your brain when it feels old;
Soak your soul in the malt of living
    To warm your heart, when hearts are cold.

Let the merchants sweat for lucre
    To provide your farewell niche;
Hoard your joy in life and loving,
    Then, God bless you, you'll die rich!

DEDICATORY HOUSE BLESSING

Master of Life:
We now dedicate to Thy service
And to the service of these, our friends,
This new house for their home.

We pray Thee to bless this roof;
May it kindly shelter them!
Bless these floors.
Grant that soon they will be well over-written
With the hieroglyphics made by the heels
Of little children, friends and neighbors.

Bless these windows which invite
The entrance of Thy sun and air.
Bless these doors; grant that they ever swing
Wide, alike to friend and wayfarer.

And doubly bless, O Lord, this hearthstone
Around which centers the life of this family.
May the fires which warm their bodies
Kindle good cheer in their hearts.

Bless this, the water which refreshes them!
Bless this, the bread which nourishes them!

As an especial mark of Thy favour,
Grant to this chimney a swallow,
To these eaves a martin
To garner insect pests from the air.

Send to this fountain a dove and a songbird,
To these fruit trees myriad warblers
To keep them clean of slugs and aphis.

Send here, O Lord, the loveliest of Thy flower faces
To enrich these lives with their beauty.
Grant that the bees swarm in this orchard;
That the butterflies, Silver Spot and Ajax, Turnus and Monarch,
Act as Thy messengers in pollen bearing.

For these, our friends, we earnestly implore these blessings.
    Amen.

INSCRIPTIONS FOR MANTELS OVER FIREPLACES
The three following are in Mrs. Porter's home in Bel-Air.

In her study:

Mother Mary seek the King.
Ask of Him a matchless thing;

Grant to this, my working place,
A wealth of wings and flower grace.

In her library:

We ask, dear Lord, a friendly fire,
A starry roof where song birds nest;
A flower to grow, a book to love,
And faithful friends to share our rest.

In her reception room:

The smallest fire even is greater by far
Than the vast dome of heaven, heaped with star on star.
Though I have only ashes for my brief delight,
All the sky is jealous of me many a night.

*A separate typescript has the title, "A Prayer," with an additional line at the beginning:
"Grant me, Dear Lord":*

A fire to warm my hearth,
A roof against the rain,
A loaf, a book, a flower,
And the friend who comes again.

We beg, dear Lord, the song of wings,
A starry roof above us,
Windows framing flowers and trees,
And all the friends who love us.

A fire I crave to toast my soles,
A roof when chilly rain descends,
Windows to let the sun shine in,
And willing doors to welcome friends.

For seaside homes:

Red-gold drift flame our hearts to cheer,
White wings of swallows o'er blue seas,

A book to love, a flower to grow,
We thank Thee, Lord, for our hearts' ease.

Drift me a blue flame azure sea,
Swift flights of swallows to their nest,
A book to love, a flower to grow,
We thank Thee Lord for this our rest.

A CHRISTMAS PRAYER

We thank thee, Lord, for Christmas cheer,
For loving faces we hold dear,
For turkey-birds and shining trees,
And thoughtful gifts that greatly please.

Bless every soul with us today,
And doubly bless friends far away.
Fill our hearts in joyful measure,
And grant a year of work and pleasure.

CYMBALS

A proud woman
Is the tall, slender tulip tree;
White flowers with hearts of gold
Shine in her hair.

When she beats her leafy cymbals
In curved strokes,
Lovingly—
She is a Salvation Army Lass
Calling on devious folk
To come back to God.

FOR A YOUNG GIRL'S AUTOGRAPH ALBUM

Go, little book, and fat thy pages,
With words of wisdom from the sages;
That you may be extremely nice,
Add here and there a jest, for spice.
And in a few of these autographs,
Be sure to hide some hearty laughs.

Thus will you give your owner pleasure,
And be to her a perfect treasure.

THE LIGHTS OF LINCOLN PARK

Los Angeles is a saucy jade,
    Shaking down her golden hair,
To veil the splendour of her face,
    High set on mountains fair.

Her lips are sweet pomegranate bloom,
    Her fingers beckoning canyons meet,
Her knees in radiant gardens bend,
    The sea frolics at her feet.

Her great heart beats with pulsing throes,
    Her million small hearts feel,
The brocades of her ruffled skirts,
    All tropic wealth reveal.

She wears upon her eagre breast,
    An emerald of wondrous green,
Quaint carved with oak and pepper tree,
    With swamp and lillied lake serene.

A jewel raying diamond lights,
    Like fallen stars smiting the dark.
Lean low and tell me, Father Abraham,
    Don't you truly love your park?

NOTES

1. Dahlke-Scott, Deborah, and Michael Prewitt, "A Writer's Crusade to Portray the Spirit of the Limberlost," *Smithsonian* 7 (Apr. 1976): 64–69 repr. in *Backpacker* 4 (Aug. 1976): 28–29, 31, 63, 65–66, as "Elder of the Tribe: Gene Stratton-Porter."

2. These page proofs include "For You!" "The Wine of Life Pitcher," "Promises," "Blue-eyed Mary," "Magic," "Our Lord's Candles," "The Quest for 'Three Birds,'" "The Bells I Hear," and the shorter version of "Symbols."

3. This set of galleys includes "Peter's Flowers," "For You!" "Sweet, Make Magic . . ." ("Magic" in *A Collection . . .*), "Escape," "Ox-heart Cherries," "The Pitcher" (a variant of "The Wine of Life Pitcher"), "Pacoima's Racing Waters," "Desire," "Fulfillment,"

"Apprehension," "Abandonment," "The Bells I Hear," "My Beachcomber," "Inscriptions for Mantels," "Field o' My Dreams," "The Quest for 'Three Birds'" (again, the title is different from that of the version in *A Collection* . . .), "Dedicatory House Blessing," "Our Lord's Candles," "Bread and Milk," "Heart of the World," "Promises," "Ode to Walt Whitman" (a fragment of "Old Walt" in typescript and elsewhere), "Babes o' the Woods," "The Miser," "Blue-eyed Mary," "A Christmas Prayer," and "Oh Lord, Lady!"

4. Quoted in John Chase Bussell, *The Technique of Gene Stratton-Porter's Novels*, ed. David MacLean (Decatur, Ind.: Americana Books, 1993), 148. Bussell states that *I Live Again* was actually published (xii); however, no copy of such a book has turned up.

5. For the present text, I have selected the versions of the poems which appear to represent Porter's latest modifications. Because the "I Live Again" galleys are clearly unedited proofs, obvious typographical errors there and elsewhere have been silently corrected.

6. *Good Housekeeping* 79 (Oct. 1924): 37, 152, 154, 157–63; *Tales You Won't Believe*, (Garden City, N.Y.: Doubleday, Page, 1925), 155–80.

7. Quoted in Meehan, *Lady of the Limberlost*, 248.

Appendix

Alphabetical Listing of Poems

BOOKS BY
GENE STRATTON-PORTER

Nature Books
THE SONG OF THE CARDINAL
FRIENDS IN FEATHERS
BIRDS OF THE BIBLE
MUSIC OF THE WILD
MOTHS OF THE LIMBERLOST
MORNING FACE
HOMING WITH THE BIRDS

Nature Stories
FRECKLES
A GIRL OF THE LIMBERLOST
AT THE FOOT OF THE RAINBOW
THE HARVESTER
LADDIE
MICHAEL O'HALLORAN
A DAUGHTER OF THE LAND
HER FATHER'S DAUGHTER
THE FIRE BIRD

Detail from endpaper of *The Fire Bird*. Courtesy of Doubleday, Page; decorations by Lee Thayer.

Selected Bibliography

WORKS BY GENE STRATTON-PORTER

Information about first publication appears here. Many of Gene Stratton-Porter's books have been reprinted one or more times.

FICTION

At the Foot of the Rainbow. New York: Outing Publishing, 1907.

A Daughter of the Land. Garden City, N.Y.: Doubleday, Page, 1918.

Freckles. New York: Doubleday, Page, 1904.

A Girl of the Limberlost. New York: Doubleday, Page, 1909.

The Harvester. Garden City, N.Y.: Doubleday, Page, 1911.

Her Father's Daughter. Garden City, N.Y.: Doubleday, Page, 1921.

The Keeper of the Bees. Garden City, N.Y.: Doubleday, Page, 1925. Serialized in *McCall's*, February–September 1925.

Laddie: A True Blue Story. Garden City, N.Y.: Doubleday, Page, 1913.

The Magic Garden. Garden City, N.Y.: Doubleday, Page, 1927. Serialized in *McCall's*, October 1926–March 1927.

Michael O'Halloran. Garden City, N.Y.: Doubleday, Page, 1915.

The Song of the Cardinal. Indianapolis: Bobbs-Merrill, 1903.

The White Flag. Garden City, N.Y.: Doubleday, Page, 1923. Serialized in *Good Housekeeping*, April–November 1923.

POETRY

"A Collection of Poems" (unpublished manuscript), 1920.

The Fire Bird. Garden City, N.Y.: Doubleday, Page, 1922.

Jesus of the Emerald. Garden City, N.Y.: Doubleday, Page, 1923.

"I Live Again" (unpublished manuscript), ca. 1937.

Nonfiction

Birds of the Bible. Cincinnati, Ohio: Jennings and Graham, 1909.

Friends in Feathers. (Revised and enlarged edition of *What I Have Done with Birds*) Garden City, N.Y.: Doubleday, Page, 1917.

Homing with the Birds. Garden City, N.Y.: Doubleday, Page, 1919.

Let Us Highly Resolve. Garden City, N.Y.: Doubleday, Page, 1927. A selection of essays previously published in *McCall's* as "Gene Stratton-Porter's Page," January 1922–December 1927.

Moths of the Limberlost. Garden City, N.Y.: Doubleday, Page, 1912.

Music of the Wild. Cincinnati, Ohio: Jennings and Graham, 1910.

Tales You Won't Believe. Garden City, N.Y.: Doubleday, Page, 1925. Serialized in *Good Housekeeping,* January 1924–February 1925.

What I Have Done with Birds. Indianapolis: Bobbs-Merrill, 1907. Serialized in *Ladies' Home Journal,* April–August 1906.

Wings. Garden City, N.Y.: Garden City Publishing, 1923. A reissue of parts of *What I Have Done with Birds, Friends in Feathers,* and *Homing with the Birds.*

Selected Magazine Publications

"Am I My Brother's Keeper?" *McCall's* 51 (February 1924): 2, 108, 109.

"Blue-eyed Mary." *Good Housekeeping* 72 (May 1921): 52.

"Books for Busy People." *McCall's* 51 (January 1924): 2, 28, 74.

"Euphorbia." (Part I) *Good Housekeeping* 76 (January 1923): 10–13, 115–21.

"Euphorbia." (Part II) *Good Housekeeping* 76 (February 1923): 24–27, 121–22, 125–26, 128–31.

"Euphorbia." (Part III) *Good Housekeeping* 76 (March 1923): 42–45, 122, 125–26, 128.

"Field o' My Dreams." *Outdoor America* 3 (December 1924): 26–27.

"Gene Stratton-Porter's Page: Advice for Aspiring Poets." *McCall's* 54 (March 1927): 142.

"Gene Stratton-Porter's Page: Choosing Words." *McCall's* 54 (October 1926): 2.

"Gene Stratton-Porter's Page: Conveniences for the Cook." *McCall's* 50 (September 1923): 2, 62.

"Gene Stratton-Porter's Page: Division of Labor in the Home." *McCall's* 54 (September 1927): 4.

"Gene Stratton-Porter's Page: For the Newlyweds." *McCall's* 53 (February 1926): 2, 76.

"Gene Stratton-Porter's Page: The Healing Influence of Gardens." *McCall's* 55 (December 1927): 120.

"Gene Stratton-Porter's Page: How I Write." *McCall's* 53 (May 1926): 2, 117.

"Having the Courage of Your Convictions." *McCall's* 51 (June 1924): 2, 26, 28, 68, 74, 93.

"Hidden Treasures: Moths of the Limberlost." *Country Life in America* 22 (June 1912): 29–36, 60, 62, 64.

"How to Make a Home." *McCall's* 49 (May 1922): 2, 65.

"Let Us Go Back to Poetry." *Good Housekeeping* 80 (April 1925): 34–35, 194–96, 199, 200.

"My Life and My Books." *Ladies' Home Journal* 23 (September 1916): 13, 80–81.
"My Work and My Critics." *The Bookman* 49 (February 1916): 147–55.
"No Lazy Man Can Make a Garden." *McCall's* 49 (June 1922): 2.
"Our Thanks." *McCall's* 52 (November 1924): 2, 81, 82, 92.
"Peter's Flowers." *Red Cross Magazine* (April 1919): 3–4.
"Symbols." *Good Housekeeping* 72 (January 1921): 12.
"Tales You Won't Believe: The Fire Bird." *Good Housekeeping* 79 (December 1924): 26–27, 178–83.
"Tales You Won't Believe: The Miracle Moth." *Good Housekeeping* 78 (June 1924): 34–35, 179–84.
"Tales You Won't Believe: The Search for 'Three Birds.'" *Good Housekeeping* 79 (October 1924): 37, 152, 154, 157–63.
"What My Father Meant to Me." *American Magazine* 99 (February 1925): 23, 70, 72, 76.
"Whitmore's Bull." *McCall's* 53 (June 1926): 8–9, 84, 102, 103.
"Why I Always Wear My Rose-Colored Glasses." *American Magazine* 88 (August 1919): 36–37, 112, 114, 117–18, 121.

OTHER

After the Flood. Indianapolis, Ind.: Bobbs-Merrill, 1911. A limited edition of short stories for children.
"A Limberlost Invitation." In *An Invitation to You and Your Folks from Jim and Some More of the Home Folks.* Compiled by George Ade for Indiana Historical Commission (Indianapolis, Ind.: Bobbs-Merrill, 1916), 7.
[Program] *Birds of the Limberlost Especially Prepared for Katherine Minahan.* New York: Doubleday, Page, 1914.
Morning Face. Garden City, N.Y.: Doubleday, Page, 1916.

SECONDARY SOURCES

Bailey, Flossie Enyart. *Pioneer Days in the Wabash Valley, with a Review of the Life of Gene Stratton-Porter.* Logansport, Ind.: Hendricks Bros., 1933.
Bakerman, Jane S. "Gene Stratton-Porter: What Price the Limberlost?" *Old Northwest* 3 (June 1977), 173–84.
Birkelo, Cheryl. "*The Harvester* and the Natural Bounty of Gene Stratton-Porter." In Thomas S. Edwards and Elizabeth A. De Wolfe, eds., *Such News of the Land: U.S. Women Nature Writers.* Hanover, N.H.: University Press of New England, 2001, 68–74, 260–61.
Birkelo, Cheryl Sahm. "Allure and Appreciation of Natural History in the Writings of Gene Stratton-Porter." Master's thesis, South Dakota State University, 2000.
Bussell, John Chase. *The Technique of Gene Stratton-Porter's Novels.* Edited by David G. MacLean. Decatur, Ind.: Americana Books, 1993.
Cooper, Frederic Taber. "The Popularity of Gene Stratton-Porter." *The Bookman* 41 (August 1915), 670–71.

Dahlke-Scott, Deborah, and Michael Prewitt. "A Writer's Crusade to Portray the Spirit of the Limberlost." *Smithsonian* 7 (April 1976): 64–69. Reprinted in *Backpacker* 4 (August 1976): 28–29, 31, 63, 65–66, as "Elder of the Tribe: Gene Stratton-Porter."

Dawald, Earl E. *The Lady of Limberlost Land*. Geneva, Ind.: Economy Printing Concern, 1951.

Fussell, Paul. *The Great War and Modern Memory*. New York: Oxford University Press, 1975.

Gene Stratton-Porter: Best Seller. Fort Wayne, Ind.: Public Library of Fort Wayne and Allen County, 1953.

Hunt, Caroline C. "Gene Stratton-Porter." *Four Women Writers for Children: 1868–1918. DLB Documentary Series: An Illustrated Chronicle*. Detroit, Mich.: Gale Research, 1996, 205–60.

Inness, Sherrie A., and Diana Royer. Introduction. In *Breaking Boundaries: New Perspectives on Women's Regional Writing*. Iowa City: Iowa University Press, 1997, 1–16.

King, Rollin Patterson. *Gene Stratton-Porter: A Lovely Light*. Chicago: Adams Press, 1979.

Lindsay-Squier, Emma. "The Lady from the Limberlost." *Los Angeles Times*, June 11, 1922.

Long, Judith Reick. *Gene Stratton-Porter: Novelist and Naturalist*. Indianapolis: Indiana Historical Society, 1990.

MacLean, David G. *Gene Stratton-Porter: A Bibliography & Collector's Guide*. Decatur, Ind.: Americana Books, 1976.

———. *Gene Stratton-Porter: A Short Biography & Collector's Guide to First Editions*. Decatur, Ind.: Americana Books, 1987.

———, ed. *Gene Stratton-Porter Remembered . . . Reprints of Selected Articles*. Series of six. Decatur, Ind.: Americana Books, 1987, 1990.

Mann, Ruth J. "Botanical Remedies from Gene Stratton Porter's *The Harvester*." *Journal of the History of Medicine* (October 1975): 367–75.

Maule, Harry E. "Mrs. Porter's first Book for Children." *Book News Monthly* 35 (December 1916): 125–26.

Meehan, Jeannette Porter. *The Lady of the Limberlost: The Life and Letters of Gene Stratton-Porter*. Garden City, N.Y.: Doubleday, Doran, 1928.

———. "Life and Letters of Gene Stratton-Porter." *McCall's* 55 (February 1928): 18–19, 88, 90–92; 55 (March 1928): 27–28, 102–6; 56 (April 1928): 39, 119–20, 123; 56 (May 1928): 36, 120–22.

———. "Memories of My Mother." *McCall's* 53 (December 1925): 12–13, 74.

Obuchowski, Mary DeJong. "Gene Stratton-Porter: Early Environmentalist." *Nature Study* 42 (October 1988): 3–5.

———. "Gene Stratton-Porter: Women's Advocate." *Midamerica* 17 (1990): 74–82. Rpt. *Children's Literature Review* 87. Detroit, Mich.: Gale Research, 2003, 116–71.

Phelps, William Lyon. "The Why of the Best Seller." *The Bookman* 54 (December 1921): 298–302.

Phillips, Anne K. "Gene Stratton-Porter." In *Dictionary of Literary Biography 221: American Women Prose Writers 1870–1920*. Detroit. Mich.: Gale, 2000, 332–338.

Plum, Sydney Landon, ed. *Coming Through the Swamp: The Nature Writings of Gene Stratton-Porter*. Salt Lake City: University of Utah Press, 1996.

———. "Gene Stratton Porter." *American Nature Writers* 2. Edited by John Elder. New York: Scribner, 1996, 877–91.

Richards, Bertrand F. *Gene Stratton-Porter: A Literary Examination*. Boston: Twayne, 1980.

Ryan, Barbara. "'Wherever I am Living' The Lady of the Limberlost Resituates." *Breaking Boundaries: New Perspectives on Women's Regional Writing*. Edited by Sherrie A. Inness and Diana Royer. Iowa City: University of Iowa Press, 1997, 162–79.

Shumaker, Arthur W. *A History of Indiana Literature: With Emphasis on the Authors of Imaginative Works Who Commenced Writing Prior to World War II*. Indianapolis: Indiana Historical Bureau, 1962.

S. F. E. *Gene Stratton-Porter: A Little Story of the Life and Ideals of the Bird Woman*. Garden City, N.Y.: Doubleday, Page, 1915. [Attributed variously to Eugene Francis Saxton, Samuel F. Ewart, and Samuel Frank Everett, the latter according to a letter in the Carnegie Public Library from Jeannette Meehan dated Jan. 1966.]

Simon, George A. "Is This an Authentic Portrait of Christ?" *The American Patriot* (April 1915): 1.